国家社科基金重大招标课题（教育学）

"建设教育强国的国际经验与中国路径研究"

（VGA180002）阶段性成果

中国教育智库评价报告

（2020年版）

刘大伟 周洪宇 著

中国社会科学出版社

图书在版编目(CIP)数据

中国教育智库评价报告：2020 年版 / 刘大伟，周洪宇著. —北京：中国社会科学出版社，2020.6
ISBN 978 - 7 - 5203 - 6614 - 4

Ⅰ.①中… Ⅱ.①刘…②周… Ⅲ.①教育事业—研究报告—中国—2020 Ⅳ.①G52

中国版本图书馆 CIP 数据核字（2020）第 094647 号

出 版 人	赵剑英
责任编辑	范晨星
责任校对	张依婧
责任印制	王 超

出 版	中国社会科学出版社
社 址	北京鼓楼西大街甲 158 号
邮 编	100720
网 址	http://www.csspw.cn
发 行 部	010 - 84083685
门 市 部	010 - 84029450
经 销	新华书店及其他书店

印 刷	北京明恒达印务有限公司
装 订	廊坊市广阳区广增装订厂
版 次	2020 年 6 月第 1 版
印 次	2020 年 6 月第 1 次印刷

开 本	710×1000 1/16
印 张	11.75
插 页	2
字 数	155 千字
定 价	59.00 元

凡购买中国社会科学出版社图书，如有质量问题请与本社营销中心联系调换
电话：010 - 84083683
版权所有　侵权必究

目　　录

一　项目背景 ……………………………………………… (1)

二　项目评价的目的、原则和方法 ……………………… (4)
　（一）明确教育智库评价的目的 ……………………… (4)
　（二）确立教育智库评价的原则 ……………………… (5)
　（三）运用科学的教育智库评价方法 ………………… (7)

三　2019年中国教育智库评价与排名 …………………… (8)
　（一）评价指标 ………………………………………… (8)
　（二）评价程序 ………………………………………… (9)
　（三）评价结果 ………………………………………… (11)
　（四）影响力分项评价 ………………………………… (16)
　（五）评价结果分析 …………………………………… (17)

四　2019年中国教育智库关注热点问题 ………………… (21)
　（一）教育现代化与教育治理 ………………………… (21)
　（二）教育法治化 ……………………………………… (24)

（三）立德树人 …………………………………………（26）
　　（四）教师减负 …………………………………………（27）
　　（五）教育国际化 ………………………………………（28）

五　2019年中国教育智库的发展特点 ……………………（30）
　　（一）咨政建言愈发有效 ………………………………（30）
　　（二）合作建设愈发多元 ………………………………（33）
　　（三）成果报告愈发专业 ………………………………（37）
　　（四）社会影响愈发扩大 ………………………………（39）

六　中国教育智库高质量发展的问题 ………………………（42）
　　（一）认识跟不上问题依然存在 ………………………（42）
　　（二）人才跟不上问题愈加明显 ………………………（45）
　　（三）管理不适应问题亟待破解 ………………………（46）
　　（四）传播不适应问题尚需改善 ………………………（48）

七　中国教育智库高质量发展的建议 ………………………（51）
　　（一）进一步提升各方对教育智库的认识 ……………（51）
　　（二）进一步加强教育智库人才的培养 ………………（53）
　　（三）进一步深化教育智库管理体制机制改革 ………（54）
　　（四）进一步扩大教育智库传播渠道与范围 …………（56）

附录1　项目组研究大事记（2019.1—2019.12） …………（57）

附录2　长江教育研究院（CERI）简介 ……………………（58）

附录3：华中师范大学教育治理与智库研究院(ETTG)简介 …… (60)

附录4：建设好社会智库 助推国家治理现代化 …………… (62)

附录5：教育智库如何做好公共外交 ………………………… (66)

后　记 ……………………………………………………………… (70)

Contents

Chapter 1 Background of the Project ·········· (75)

Chapter 2 Purposes, Principles and Methods of the Project ·········· (80)
  (1) Clarify the purpose of education think tank evaluation ······ (80)
  (2) Establishing principles of education think tank evaluation ·········· (81)
  (3) Using scientific methods of education think tank evaluation ·········· (84)

Chapter 3 China Education Think Tank Evaluation and 2019 Rankings ·········· (86)
  (1) Indicators of evaluation ·········· (86)
  (2) Procedures of evaluation ·········· (88)
  (3) Results of evaluation ·········· (90)
  (4) Influence evaluation by item ·········· (95)
  (5) Data analysis of think tanks selected for CETTE ·········· (97)

Chapter 4　Main Research Topics of Education Think Tanks in 2019 ……………………………………………（102）

（1）Education modernization and educational governance ……（103）
（2）Education legal system construction …………………………（106）
（3）Cultivating ideals of talents ……………………………………（108）
（4）Reducing burden of teachers …………………………………（110）
（5）Education internationalization …………………………………（112）

Chapter 5　Characteristics of Chinese Education Think Tanks in 2019 ……………………………………………（114）

（1）More effective advice and consultation ……………………（114）
（2）More diverse collaborations …………………………………（119）
（3）More professional research reports ………………………（126）
（4）Greater social influence ………………………………………（128）

Chapter 6　Problems in the Process of Education Think Tank Development ………………………………………（134）

（1）Lack of understanding …………………………………………（135）
（2）The unsatisfactory quality of professional researchers ……（138）
（3）The problem of management mechanism …………………（141）
（4）The problem of communication and outreaching …………（144）

Chapter 7　Suggestions for High-quality Development of Chinese education Think Tanks ……………………（148）

（1）Further enhance knowledge of education think tanks ……（148）
（2）Further strengthen the cultivation of education think tank talents ……………………………………………………（151）

(3) Further deepen the reform of management mechanism ...... (153)

(4) Further expand the channels and scope of education think tank communication and outreaching .... (156)

Appendix 1 Events of this Project in 2019 .... (158)

Appendix 2 Brief Introduction of Changjiang Education Research Institute (CERI) .... (159)

Appendix 3 Brief introduction of Research and Evaluation Center for Educational Think Tank and Governance (ETTG) .... (161)

Appendix 4 Constructing Social Think Tanks and Promote National Governance Modernization .... (165)

Appendix 5 How Education Think Tanks Engage with Public Diplomacy .... (172)

一　项目背景

教育是国之大计，党之大计。2019年是中华人民共和国成立70周年，也是全面建成小康社会、实现第一个百年奋斗目标的关键之年。同时，2019年还是全面贯彻落实全国教育大会精神的开局之年，也是加快推进落实《中国教育现代化2035》、建设教育强国的奠基之年。2019年伊始，教育部及各省市相继召开全国教育工作会议及各省市教育大会，贯彻、推进、落实习近平总书记在全国教育大会上对教育工作的指示。2019年10月底，党的十九届四中全会审议通过了《中共中央关于坚持和完善中国特色社会主义制度、推进国家治理体系和治理能力现代化若干重大问题的决定》，提出要"坚持和完善中国特色社会主义制度、推进国家治理体系和治理能力现代化"。作为国家治理现代化的一部分，教育治理现代化的重要助推器之一就是教育智库，它对完善中国特色新型智库体系，促进党和政府科学民主依法决策，深化国家改革开放，提升国家软实力做出了实实在在的贡献。在这一历史背景下，各方教育智库开始积极融入国家发展战略，将教育强国的部署转化为实际行动，不断推动教育治理体系和治理能力现代化。这其中，既有对接"四点一线一面"国家宏观战略研究的高端教育智库，也有以地方教育发展为研究目标，推进区域教育发展与社会融合的地方教育智库，这些教育智库共同为教育强国的目标献计献策，提供强大的智力保障。为更好地促进各类教育智库健康有序发展，实现以评促建的目标，以便为重现《中国教育现代化2035》部署的任务提供更多的智力支持，本项目组继续推进中国教育智库评价研究。本报告是《中国教育智库评价SFAI研究报告》年度报告系列的第二本。项目组以建设中国教育智库数据库为手段，搜集整理国内各教育智库的基本情况，研判当前中国教育智库发展存在的问题，寻找解决问题的路径与方法，同时辅之以评价入选数据库的教育智库的结构、功能、成果和影响力。项目组希望能够不断完善国内教育智库数据库的基本数据，最终成为中国教育智库的数据分析中心。

2018年11月10日，项目组在北京首次发布《中国教育智库评价SFAI研究报告（2018）》，研究报告总结了自2013年起，各教育智库在习近平总书记关于智库的重要论述基础上开展的各项工作，梳理了中国教育智库建设存在的问题并提出了相应对策，同时还对入选数据库的各教育智库进行了分析，遴选出一批具有良好成果和影响力的核心智库和入选智库，引发了教育智库界的强烈反响。进入数据库遴选智库的相关单位纷纷刊发新闻报道，形成了良好的社会反响，构建了"评价—建设"的良好互动机制。这其中，有教育部人文社会科学重点研究基地的东北师范大学中国农村教育发展研究院、西南大学西南民族教育与心理研究中心、南京师范大学道德教育研究所等师范类高校教育智库；有南京大学高等教育研究与评价中心、宁波大学海洋教育研究中心等综合类高校教育智库；有上海师范大学国际与比较教育研究院等国际共建类教育智库；还有成都市教育科学研究院、南京市教育科学研究所等地方教育科研院所，当然，更多的还是如淮北师范大学安徽省高校管理大数据研究中心、江苏大学教育政策研究所、天津科技大学天津市教育发展研究中心、唐山师范学院京津冀高等教育发展研究中心、东莞理工学院高等教育研究所等地方高校教育智库。这些教育智库对评价报告的肯定，成为本项目进一步深化研究的内在动力。

2019年4月27日，项目组在不断完善改进的基础上，由中国社会科学出版社出版了《中国教育智库评价 SFAI 研究报告（2019年版）》（中英文双语版），并在北京召开了新书发布会暨首届中国教育智库建设论坛，邀请教育部社科司相关司长、中国教育科学研究院、北京师范大学中国教育与社会发展研究院、上海师范大学联合国教师教育中心、华中师范大学教育治理与智库研究院、南京师范大学道德教育研究所、南京大学高等教育研究与评价中心、长江教育研究院等重要教育智库的负责人参会并发表演讲。会后，项目组决定进一步调整完善指标体系，调研走访各类教育智库，借助 CETTE（China Education Think Tank Evaluation）平台搜集整理各种信息数据，以主客观相结合的评价方法，在数据的基础上综合业内专家的意见，最终完成了本年度的《中国教育智库评价报告》。

二　项目评价的目的、原则和方法

要实现"构建和完善现代教育决策服务体系"这一目标，本项目组希望通过评建结合，合理有效地发挥"以评促建"作用，全面推动教育智库的良性发展。

（一）明确教育智库评价的目的

教育智库评价的目的归根结底是要助力实现中国教育现代化。《中国教育现代化2035》提出"到2035年，总体实现教育现代化，迈入教育强国行列，推动我国成为学习大国、人力资源强国和人才强国"这一总体奋斗目标，并围绕这一目标重点部署了十大战略任务。要实现总体目标并落实十大任务，教育智库的作用是非常重要的。教育智库不仅能够聚才、育才，实现人才强国目标，而且还能够通过构建现代教育决策服务体系，为每一大任务的落实提供具体抓手和实现路径。所以，从实现《中国教育现代化2035》目标计，我们要借助评价总结各教育智库建设的经验，发现教育智库建设中的问题，探寻破解问题的方法与路径，而并非以简单的评价排行榜来营造虚假的教育智库繁荣景象。

从这一角度来说，教育智库评价体系的目的就是希望能够通过评价，推出一批典型性教育智库，总结他们发展的经验，共同商讨解决发展中的问题，推而广之，助力形成更多更好的教育智库，在宏观决策、一线实践为《中国教育现代化2035》目标的实现提供全方位的支持。

（二）确立教育智库评价的原则

首先，坚持理论与实践相统一的原则。教育智库与其他智库相比较还是存在一定的特殊性。它既"顶天"，要考虑到教育决策的宏观布局；也"立地"，要结合各大、中、小学的实际教育教学情况。所以，对教育智库的评价不仅仅是看这一智库在咨政建言方面发挥了多少作用，也要考虑其对中国一线教育改革实践产生的实际价值。项目组始终遵循理论与实践相结合的原则，充分考虑了致力于基层教育实践并发挥重大影响和作用的教育智库，如各级各类教科院所等一些单位。实际上，基层教科院所的实践以及对当地教育行政部门产生的影响，往往是一些综合性智库评价榜单所忽略的。

其次，坚持内涵与形式相统一的原则。习近平总书记批评了有些智库"重形式传播、轻内容创新问题"，"还有的流于搭台子、请名人、办论坛等形式主义的做法"，所以我们在评价教育智库时，坚决贯彻落实习近平总书记的指示，强调内涵与形式相统一的原则，既关注教育智库的影响力，也极为关注教育智库的内涵建设。我们始终秉承"结构—功能"理论，除去考察教育智库产生的"成果力""影响力"等功能之外，我们还重点考察了教育智库的结构，如教育智库的整体框架、日常工作活动等；不仅关注教育智库的实体化发展进程，也关注其成果的研究质量、内容创新，其目标就是为了彻底避免"皮包智库"成为教育智库评价榜单中的一员。

坚持严格筛选与鼓励发展相统一的原则。教育智库的建设发展是一个稳步推进的过程。2016年，时任教育部副部长郝平在全国教育科学研究院（所）工作会议上指出，"未来5年，是彰显教育科研作用、做大做强教育智库的黄金时期"[①]。近四年以来，教育智库的数量在不断增加，但放眼建设教育强国这一目标，现在的教育智库数量及质量与未来需求还是存在较大的差距。因而，在评价过程中，项目组坚持严格筛选与鼓励发展相结合，剔除了一些名不副实的所谓"教育智库"机构，但也遴选了一些刚刚起步正在发展的教育智库，特别是老少边穷地区的教育智库。项目组认为，通过培育、鼓励、发展这些教育智库，有助于提高他们在政策研究方面的积极性，并为破解中国教育发展不平衡不充分问题提供更准确的决策咨询。

坚持立足中国与全球视野相统一的原则。智库的五大功能当中包含有"智库外交"这一功能，习近平总书记也多次强调智库外交的作用和价值。因此，在教育智库评价过程中，必须要坚持立足中国与全球视野相统一，在深入了解中国本土教育情况的基础上，鼓励教育智库积极参与国际同行交流，在国际机构共建、国际推广合作、海外员工聘请方面采取一些具体的举措。只有将中国教育故事讲到国际舞台，参与国际教育话题的探讨，并逐步掌握世界教育话语权，才能充分展现出中国的教育自信。因而，项目组一如既往关注"国际共建"类型的教育智库，它们将会是率先向国际教育界讲述中国教育故事的排头兵。

---

① 《中国教育报》，2016年1月15日。

（三）运用科学的教育智库评价方法

习近平总书记在全国教育大会上强调，"扭转不科学的教育评价导向，坚决克服唯分数、唯升学、唯文凭、唯论文、唯帽子的顽瘴痼疾，从根本上解决教育评价指挥棒问题"[1]。因此，项目组以"破五唯"为宗旨，通过搭建"中国教育智库评估平台"，借助网络爬虫技术多方搜集遴选智库相关信息，通过客观数据汇总分析与遴选智库实地调研相结合，同时借助业内专家的主观评判，最终以主客观评价法相结合的形式描绘出中国教育智库发展的现状。

---

[1] 《人民日报》，2018年9月11日。

三　2019年中国教育智库评价与排名

（一）评价指标

在《中国教育智库评价SFAI研究报告（2019年版）》的数据采集过程中，项目组对指标数据的采集有以下几点反馈：（1）教育智库普遍在起步发展阶段，相较于其他经济智库、政治智库的成熟度而言，教育智库在组织架构及投入保障方面明显还不够完善；（2）绝大部分教育智库不是实体化运营，所以在经费投入、体制建设等方面依赖于母体机构；（3）很多教育智库的日常工作多与母体机构重叠，很难分辨两者的差异；（4）部分自主填报数据无法核实真伪，使得第三方评估者无法辨别。以上种种，迫使项目组一是改进数据采集办法，二是调整部分指标体系，尽可能设置较为容易采集到数据的指标。指标调整后，我们与前一次研究相同，采取层次分析法和德尔菲法，对每个指标的权重进行重新测算。同时，我们还增加了参考指标，即智库成立时间。智库成立时间的长短对智库的活跃度、影响力、成果各方面也有一定的影响。

三 2019年中国教育智库评价与排名

表1　　　　　　中国教育智库评价指标体系

一级指标	二级指标	三级指标
结构指标	组织架构	理事会
		首席专家
	智库保障	经费投入
		科研人员
		制度机制
功能指标	智库工作	调研考察
		公开发行出版物
		新媒体维护
	智库活动	专题会议
		高规格论坛
成果指标	决策成果	提交内参
		提交咨询报告
	学术成果	论文
		图书
		课题
	应用成果	提供教育服务
影响力指标	决策影响力	领导批示
		咨询建言
		规划起草
	社会影响力	媒体报道
		国内合作
		成果传播
	国际影响力	海外员工
		国际合作
		国际传播
成长指标（参考指标）	成立时间	成立时间

（二）评价程序

1. 完善教育智库备选池

从2019年5月起，项目组结合中国社会科学院《中国智库综合评价 AMI 研究报告（2017）》、上海社会科学研究院发布的《2018 中国智库报告：影响力排名与政策建议》、南京大学 CTTI 数据平台、《中国智库名录 2016》等多方机构的入选智库，以及搜寻各省市活跃度较高的教育智库，特别是中西部地区的高校教育智库和全国范围的教科院所，不断扩大教育智库备选池。在经过项目组反复研讨后，将本次教育智库的备选池范围扩大至 103 家。

2. 进行部分教育智库的调研

此项工作自 2019 年年初开始展开，时间跨度为全年。项目组对上年度入选的智库及进入备选池的相关智库进行走访调研，形式既有实地调研访谈，也有借助集中会议调查访谈。由于项目组人员有限，全年共计走访调研相关教育智库 23 家。事实上，在智库实地调研这一方面，项目组认为其他智库评价体系采取的网络填报、问卷填报等方法，存在一定的数据不真实性，鉴于教育智库评价的整体体量较小，项目组拟于 2020 年进一步推进实地调研，力争跑遍遴选的教育智库。

3. 开展调查遴选工作

2019 年 8 月—10 月，项目组对原有 CETTE 平台进行改建完善，简化了输入流程。同时由南京晓庄学院信息工程学院教师组建维护团队，采取网络爬虫技术对各教育智库在 2019 年的相关信息进行采集。这其中既包括国内外相关网站中各教育智库的新闻报道，也包括中国知网中各智库的期刊论文发表及被引率等，还有全国哲学社会科学工作办公室、全国教育科学规划办等网站公布的课题数量等。最终项目组经过人工遴选，对各智库的数据汇总整理，输入 CETTE 数据库并计算加权得分。随后，项目组结合数据，借助多轮主观评价的方法，将主客观评价相结合，对中国活跃的教育智库进行打分和排名。

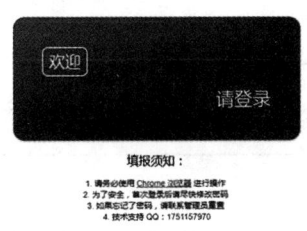

图 1　中国教育智库评估平台登录界面

4. 发布并进一步完善

2019年11月9日，项目组在北京外国语大学承办的"2019教育智库与教育治理50人圆桌论坛"上发布《中国教育智库评价报告（2019）》简版，取得了良好的社会反响。同时，项目组在会后根据各方反馈，通过电话调研、实地走访等方式进一步搜集相关教育智库的具体信息，不断完善数据库遴选智库的各项数据。

5. 专家评议

项目组基于以上成果，在南京、武汉、北京召开三次教育智库专家评议会，以及多轮次小范围的意见征询会，对教育智库的评价结果进行讨论分析。

（三）评价结果

项目组通过数据搜集整理、专家评价分析相结合的主客观评价法，遴选出2019年中国教育智库评价（CETTE）榜单。结果如下：

1. 核心教育智库

表2　　　　入选CETTE核心教育智库（政府直属类）
（按教育智库名称拼音字母排列，排名不分先后）

教育智库名称
国家教育发展研究中心
中国教育科学研究院

表3　　　　入选CETTE核心教育智库（地方教科院所类）
（按教育智库名称拼音字母排列，排名不分先后）

教育智库名称
北京教育科学研究院
重庆市教育科学研究院
广东省教育研究院
湖南省教育科学研究院
江苏省教育科学研究院
上海市教育科学研究院
浙江省教育科学研究院

表4　　　　入选CETTE核心教育智库（国际共建类）
（按教育智库名称拼音字母排列，排名不分先后）

教育智库名称
北京师范大学联合国教科文组织国际农村教育研究与培训中心（北京师范大学农村教育与农村发展研究院）
南方科技大学联合国教科文组织高等教育创新中心
上海师范大学国际与比较教育研究院（上海师范大学联合国教科文组织教师教育中心）

三 2019 年中国教育智库评价与排名 ▶▶▶

表 5　　入选 CETTE 核心教育智库（双一流高校类）

（按教育智库名称拼音字母排列，排名不分先后）

教育智库名称
北京大学中国教育财政科学研究所
北京师范大学首都教育经济研究院
北京师范大学中国教育与社会发展研究院
北京师范大学中国基础教育质量监测协同创新中心
东北师范大学中国农村教育发展研究院
华东师范大学国家教育宏观政策研究院
华东师范大学课程与教学研究所
华中师范大学教育治理与智库研究院
南京大学高等教育研究与评价中心
南京师范大学道德教育研究所
清华大学教育研究院
首都师范大学首都教育政策与法律研究院
西南大学西南民族教育与心理研究中心
浙江大学中国科教战略研究院

表 6　　入选 CETTE 核心教育智库（其他高校类）

（按教育智库名称拼音字母排列，排名不分先后）

教育智库名称
安徽师范大学安徽教育发展研究中心
广西师范大学广西民族教育发展研究中心
广州大学教育政策研究中心
海南师范大学海南教育改革与发展研究院
淮北师范大学安徽省高校管理大数据研究中心
江苏教育现代化研究院
江苏大学教育政策研究所
天津师范大学翔宇基础教育实践研究所
天津科技大学天津市教育发展研究中心
西北师范大学西北少数民族教育发展研究中心
中南民族大学少数民族教育政策与法规研究所

· 13 ·

表7　　　　入选 CETTE 核心教育智库（社会类）
（按教育智库名称拼音字母排列，排名不分先后）

教育智库名称
21 世纪教育研究院
长江教育研究院
中国教育三十人论坛

2. 来源教育智库

表8　　　　入选 CETTE 来源教育智库（地方教科院所类）
（按教育智库名称拼音字母排列，排名不分先后）

教育智库名称
成都市教育科学研究院
福建省教育科学研究所
广州市教育研究院
湖北省教育科学研究院
吉林省教育科学院
山东省教育科学研究院
深圳市教育科学研究院

表9　　　　入选 CETTE 来源教育智库（双一流高校类）
（按教育智库名称拼音字母排列，排名不分先后）

教育智库名称
北京师范大学教师教育研究中心
北京师范大学国际与比较教育研究院
北京师范大学国家职业教育研究院
复旦大学高等教育研究所
河南大学教育改革与发展研究中心
华中师范大学湖北省教育政策研究中心
华中师范大学信息化与基础教育均衡发展省部共建协同创新中心
南京师范大学教育领导与管理研究所

续表

教育智库名称
宁波大学海洋教育研究中心
陕西师范大学教育法治研究中心
陕西师范大学西部教育研究中心
上海交通大学世界一流大学研究中心
同济大学教育政策研究中心
厦门大学高等教育质量与评估研究所
中国人民大学教育立法研究基地
中国人民大学教育发展与公共政策研究中心

表10　入选 CETTE 来源教育智库（其他高校类）
（按教育智库名称拼音字母排列，排名不分先后）

教育智库名称
东莞理工学院高等教育研究所
广西师范大学东盟教育研究院
湖北大学信息化与基础教育均衡发展研究中心
湖北第二师范学院湖北教师教育研究中心
南京晓庄学院南京教育智库
天津职业技术师范大学职业教育教师研究院
唐山师范学院京津冀高等教育发展研究中心
武汉工程大学高等教育研究所

表11　入选 CETTE 来源教育智库（社会类）
（按教育智库名称拼音字母排列，排名不分先后）

教育智库名称
方略研究院
奕阳教育研究院
中华教育改进社

（四）影响力分项评价

上年度报告中的指标体系权重测算中，影响力指标达到了0.4778，本次指标体系略加调整后，影响力指标权重测算为0.4832，再次证明了智库归根到底发挥作用和价值还是体现在影响力方面。为此，本次评价过程中，我们结合数据分析和专家打分，从决策影响力、社会影响力、成果影响力三方面对当前中国教育智库进行了梳理。之所以没有考虑评估国际影响力这一点，是因为当前我国教育智库还普遍没有发挥好"公共外交"这一职能，少有教育智库走出去的实例。另外增加了成果影响力，从一级指标"成果指标"中"学术成果"方面提取数据，之所以这么考虑，是因为长期的研究成果发布传播，也会形成学术界对某一教育问题的关注，最终成为决策形成的幕后推手。具体的评价结果如下：

1. 决策影响力

表12　　　　　　　　　决策影响力排名

排名	教育智库名称
1	中国教育科学研究院
2	国家教育发展研究中心
3	北京师范大学中国教育与社会发展研究院
4	北京大学中国教育财政科学研究所
5	华东师范大学国家教育宏观政策研究院
6	长江教育研究院
7	清华大学教育研究院
8	北京师范大学联合国教科文组织国际农村教育研究与培训中心（北京师范大学农村教育与农村发展研究院）
9	东北师范大学中国农村教育发展研究院
10	上海师范大学国际与比较教育研究院（上海师范大学联合国教科文组织教师教育中心）

2. 社会影响力

表 13　　　　　　　　　社会影响力排名

排名	教育智库名称
1	长江教育研究院
2	21世纪教育研究院
3	中国教育三十人论坛
4	中国教育科学研究院
5	东北师范大学中国农村教育发展研究院
6	华东师范大学国家教育宏观政策研究院
7	北京师范大学中国基础教育质量监测协同创新中心
8	华中师范大学教育治理与智库研究院
9	北京教育科学研究院
10	中华教育改进社

3. 成果影响力

表 14　　　　　　　　　成果影响力排名

排名	教育智库名称
1	中国教育科学研究院
2	清华大学教育研究院
3	北京师范大学中国教育与社会发展研究院
4	东北师范大学中国农村教育发展研究院
5	长江教育研究院
6	华东师范大学国家教育宏观政策研究院
7	北京师范大学首都教育经济研究院
8	西南大学西南民族教育与心理研究中心
9	南京师范大学道德教育研究所
10	北京大学中国教育财政科学研究所

（五）评价结果分析

1. 教育智库地域分析

此次中国教育智库评估平台（CETTE）遴选入库的教育智库

共计74家,遍布国内北京、上海、湖北、江苏、浙江、广东、陕西、重庆等20个省市。从数量上来看,北京、湖北、上海、江苏分列前四位,这也与这四个省市的科教背景密不可分。其中,北京以20家教育智库入选遥遥领先,这也体现了北京的教育中心地位,也与北京师范大学等高校的教育智库逐步细化分类有密切关系;湖北以9家教育智库次之,主要因为华中师范大学教育治理与智库研究院在华中区域的引导作用,推动这一区域在教育智库建设方面取得了长足的进步;上海、江苏两地本就是教育强省(市),华东师范大学、上海师范大学等高校在教育智库的建设方面有着丰富的经验,而江苏省在省委宣传部的引导下,各方面智库建设都有长足的进步。

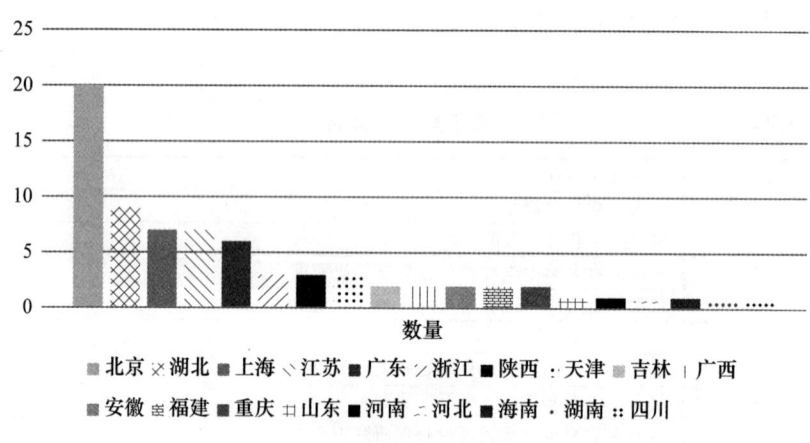

图2　中国教育智库地域分析

但统计显示,依然有十多个省市自治区还没有建立系统的、合理的、有效的教育智库。在本次调研过程中,项目组反复对一些省份进行检索,但依然找不出有代表性的教育智库,故本次遴选过程中,除去港澳台地区外,还有11个省市没有教育智库入选。这其中既有去年入选智库由于整年未能开展有效工作,成为"挂名智库"后的剔除，也有相关省市根本无法遴选出活跃智库。这些省份主要集中在我国中西部地区，这既与当地科教资源的缺乏有关，也可能与当地政府及职能部门对智库学习理解的程度有关。中西部地区教育智库的缺失，导致教育政策研究者无法有效参与教育治理能力和治理体系现代化建设的过程，会在未来进一步桎梏中西部地区教育的发展，这也将成为未来国家政策导向需要进一步改善提升的重要区域。在将来的很长一段时间里，引导中西部地区教科院所向教育智库转向，同时扶持各区域高校教育智库主动参与区域治理，将会是一个长足的生长点。

2. 教育智库类型分析

从教育智库的类型来看，高校智库仍然是最主要的组成部分。本次统计中，高校教育智库包括了国际共建教育智库、双一流高校教育智库和其他高校教育智库，共有52所，占入选智库总数的70%。而在这其中，双一流高校教育智库拥有更多的渠道报送途径，所以毫无疑问成了教育智库的最主要组成部分。而地方教科院所的转型过程依然艰难。传统意义的教科院所侧重于关注课程、教学等微观具体事宜，很少会关心区域教育改革等重大教育战略问题。调研显示，目前北京、上海、广东、江苏、重庆等教育资源较为发达的省市教科院所已经形成了教科研与教育宏观决策双轮驱动的态势，但其他地方教科院所依然还在传统研究领域开展工作。社会教育智库依然成长乏力，这与政治、经济领域社会智库的发展形成了鲜明对比。而国际共建教育智库，作为本研究报告中重要分类项，其活跃度还需要进一步提升，才能发挥其特有的国际资源。

在这一分类中，其他高校教育智库这一类别占到了26%，项目组认为这一类别教育智库将会成为推动地方教育治理的重要动力。这一类别的高校教育智库不同于双一流高校教育智库，他们

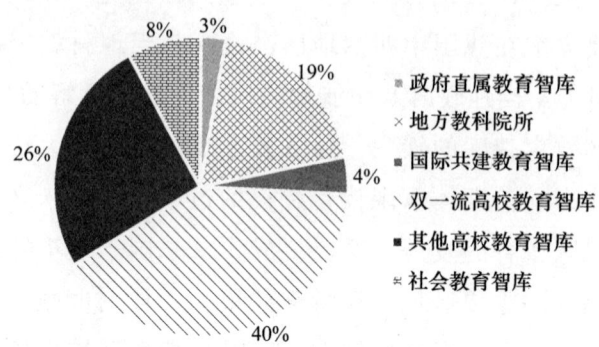

图3　中国教育智库类型分析

的着眼点更聚焦于本地的教育政策制定与教育改革推进。当前全国各地都在稳步推进落实全国教育大会精神，而各地市要落实、研究、做好做实，需要倚靠的只能是各地市区域范围以内的教育智库。所以，今后这一类别智库也会成为教育智库快速增长的突破点。

四 2019年中国教育智库关注热点问题

2019年对于中国教育具有重大意义，本年度各省市自治区相继召开省、市各级教育大会，贯彻落实中央各项教育政策，各教育智库在这一过程中积极参与治理，在咨政建言、理论创新、舆论引导、社会服务和公关外交方面发挥了重要的作用。这一年中，各类教育智库的关注热点主要集中在以下几个方面。

图4 2019年教育智库研究关注热词

（一）教育现代化与教育治理

2019年年初，中共中央、国务院印发了《中国教育现代化

2035》和《加快推进教育现代化实施方案（2018—2022年)》，引起了社会各界的强烈关注。随后，各大教育智库开展了一系列的研究，在文件解读、落地实施等环节形成了一系列的成果。在这一过程中，国家教育发展研究中心、中国教育科学研究院、北京师范大学中国教育与社会发展研究院、长江教育研究院等一系列高端教育智库相继在《光明日报》《中国教育报》[①]等重要报纸发表解读文章，在舆论引导方面起到了良好的表率。中国教育科学研究院联合全国教育科学规划领导小组办公室于2019年4月17日在北京召开"中国教育科学论坛"，聚焦落实《中国教育现代化2035》的路径研究。在理论研究方面，对《中国教育现代化2035》的政策解读及相关研究，从年初一直延续到2019年年底，体现了各教育智库对这一热点问题的持续关注，其关注点包括学前教育现代化、义务教育现代化、职业教育现代化等不同学段的现代化。2019年12月8日，中国教育三十人论坛主办了主题为"科技发展与教育变革"的年会，聚焦于科技与教育生态的变革以及科技发展给教育带来的挑战，这一年会为全年的教育现代化研究热点画上了句号。

教育现代化离不开治理体系的现代化。从年初《中国教育现代化2035》发布开始，就有教育智库关注到教育治理体系现代化的研究，并发表了相关研究成果。而伴随着2019年10月底党的十

---

① 研究统计仅为项目组遴选教育智库的研究人员，非教育遴选智库的研究成果不在统计之列，以下仅列举一二：顾明远：《新时代推进教育现代化要怎么做》，《光明日报》2019年3月5日；谈松华：《准确把握教育现代化的四个关键点》，《光明日报》2019年3月5日；张力：《如何理解2035年教育现代化目标》，《光明日报》2019年3月19日；周洪宇、刘大伟：《中国教育现代化走向新时代新目标新征程》，《中国教育报》2019年4月1日；薛二勇：《新时代推进教育现代化的新征程开启》，《人民政协报》2019年2月27日；胡娟：《高等教育现代化要破解三大难题》，《光明日报》2019年4月23日；李立国：《大学治理现代化的价值理念》，《光明日报》2019年11月19日；等等。

四 2019年中国教育智库关注热点问题 ▶▶▶

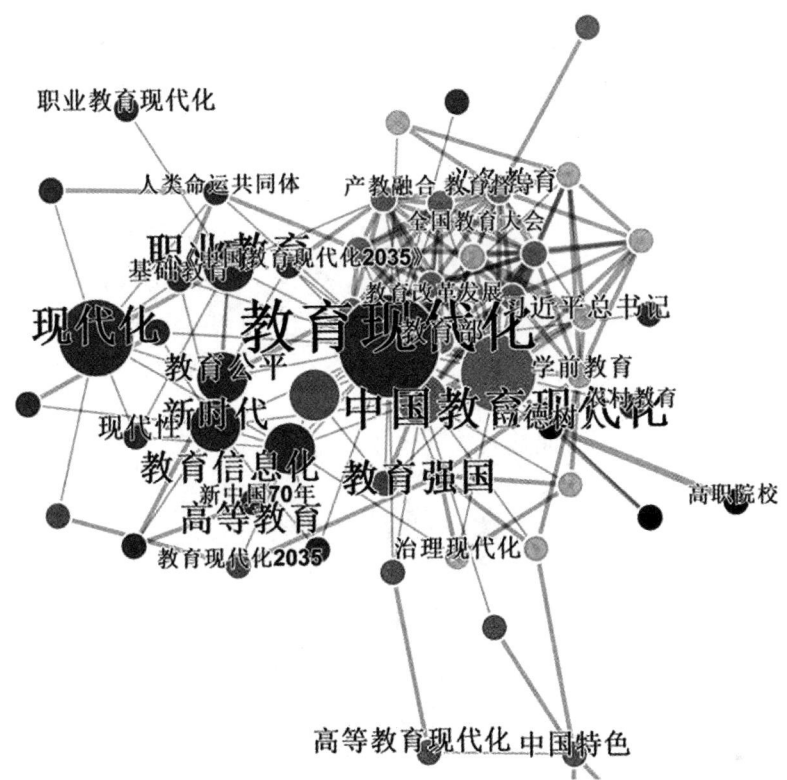

图 5　2019 年与"教育现代化"相关文章的关键词共现网络

九届四中全会的召开，各教育智库相继开展了对国家教育治理体系现代化和治理能力现代化的研究①。2019 年 11 月 9 日，长江教育研究院以"深化教育改革，加快推进教育治理体系和治理能力现代化"为主题，在北京召开"2019 教育智库与教育治理 50 人圆

---

① 相关教育智库在这一方面成果较多，仅列举一二：周洪宇：《深化教育领域"放管服"改革，加快推进教育治理现代化》，《教育研究》2019 年第 3 期；周洪宇：《加强教育科学研究 助力教育治理体系现代化》，《教育研究》2019 年第 11 期；崔保师：《新时代我国教育科学研究工作基本制度和治理体系的蓝图》，《教育研究》2019 年第 11 期；莫兰：《教育治理不仅是在学校围墙内寻求方案》，《光明日报》2019 年 11 月 19 日；邬大光：《大学治理：从经验走向科学》，《光明日报》2019 年 12 月 2 日；等等。

桌论坛",徐辉、张力、张民选、周洪宇、彭斌柏等专家学者就落实党的十九届四中全会精神畅谈教育改革措施。这一研究热点问题将会在当前及今后很长一段时间内成为各教育智库关注的重点问题。

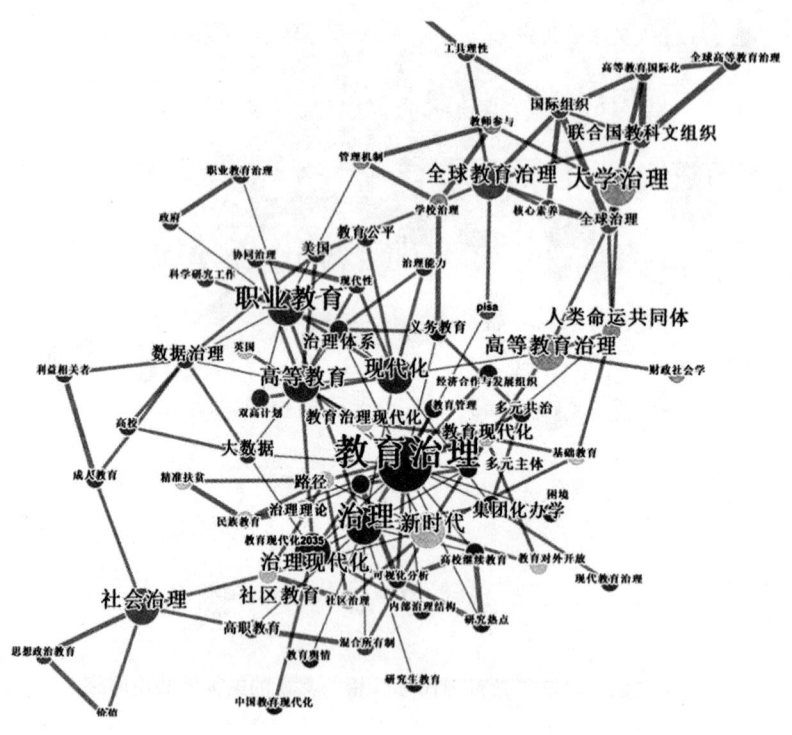

图6 2019年与"教育治理"相关文章的关键词共现网络

（二）教育法治化

2019年年初，全国教育政策法治工作会议召开，会议强调要全面推进依法治教，加快立法工作步伐，为教育改革发展提供政策法治保障。本年度中，教育法治问题最引发关注的是学前教育立法和教育惩戒权问题。2019年1月5日，北京师范大学中国教育与社会发展研究院与首都教育经济研究院联合主办了"学前教育深化改革与发展研讨会",庞丽娟、王善迈、吕玉刚、朱旭东等专家学者就学前教育管理体制、投入体制和办园体制等方面问题深入探讨。随后两会期间,担任全国人大代表的教育智库负责人如庞丽娟、周洪宇等在会议期间提议加快推动学前教育法立法以及修订《教师法》予以教师惩戒权等提案,引发了社会的广泛关注。围绕教育法治化进程问题以及涉及的具体要点,上述多家教育智库开展了深入研究,并由教育部教师工作司直接参与指导,最终形成专报、论文等多种形式成果递交相关职能部门。2019年7月,中共中央、国务院出台《关于深化教育教学改革全面提高义务教育质量的意见》,明确提出保障教师依法享有教育惩戒权。这也体现出了教育智库对教育政策影响的重要作用。

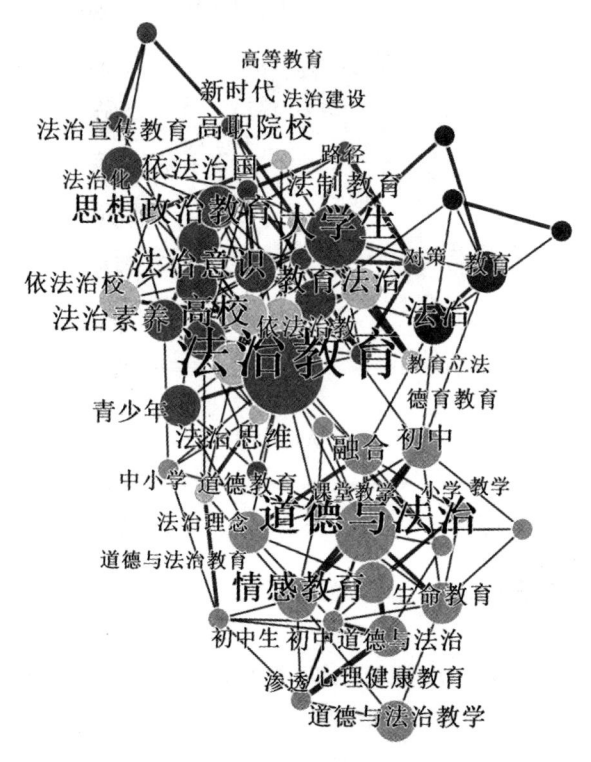

图7 2019年与"教育法治"相关文章的关键词共现网络

（三）立德树人

习近平总书记在全国教育大会上强调，要"围绕培养什么人、怎样培养人、为谁培养人这一根本问题"，"坚持立德树人，加强学校思想政治工作，推进教育改革"，"教育现代化加速推进"[①]。

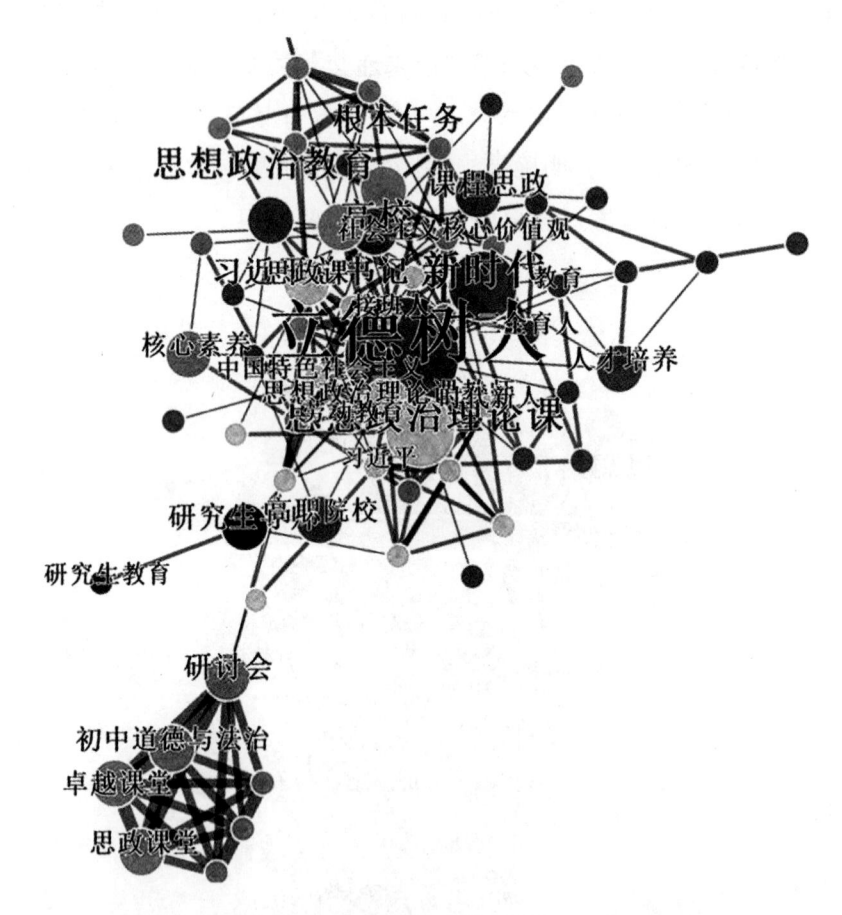

图8　2019年与"立德树人"相关文章的关键词共现网络

---

① 《人民日报》，2018年9月11日。

因而，在2019年，相关教育智库如北京师范大学中国教育与社会发展研究院、南京师范大学道德教育研究所等机构高度重视立德树人这一问题，开展各类学术研讨，发表研究成果①，在理论创新、舆论引导和社会服务三个维度充分发挥了教育智库的作用和价值。智库的呼吁也与政府的诉求相结合，推动着2019年《关于加强新时代中小学思想政治理论课教师队伍建设的意见》《关于加强和改进新时代师德师风建设的意见》等相关文件的出台，为立德树人提供了政策保障依据，也为立德树人的目标实现落实了实施路径。

（四）教师减负

2019年为中共中央提出的"基层减负年"，因而在2019年年初的全国教育工作会议上，教育部部长陈宝生强调将会花大力气为教师减负，这一提议也成了该年度教育智库关心的热点话题。为实现这一目标，教育部召开多次座谈会，邀请相关智库成员与会并发表意见。相关教育智库也系统梳理了各地教师减负的经验，学习借鉴西方发达国家在这一方面的措施，大量走访调研多地中小学校，在报纸期刊发表文章引导舆论②，并撰写相关研究专报递

---

① 相关教育智库在这一方面成果较多，仅列举一二：薛二勇：《教育持续促进人的全面发展》，《中国教育报》2019年10月8日；冯建军：《立德树人的时代内涵与实施路径》，《人民教育》2019年第18期；冯建军：《构建立德树人的系统化落实机制》，《国家教育行政学院学报》2019年第4期；周洪宇：《加强对习近平总书记关于教育的重要论述的研究阐释》，《中国高等教育》2019年第19期；等等。

② 相关教育智库在这一方面成果较多，仅列举一二：叶美金、邹大光：《减轻教师负担，拓宽发展空间》，《光明日报》2019年3月12日；邵泽斌：《教师减负：目标是增能，关键是制度》，《光明日报》2019年4月2日；王明娣、王鉴：《教师减负要做到"三回归"》，《光明日报》2019年4月2日；周洪宇：《为教师减负要从根上做起》，《光明日报》2019年10月31日；等等。

送教育部有关司局。最终，在多方共同的努力下，2019年年底，中共中央办公厅、国务院办公厅印发了《关于减轻中小学教师负担进一步营造教育教学良好环境的若干意见》，为中小学减负增能，"把宁静还给学校，把时间还给教师"。

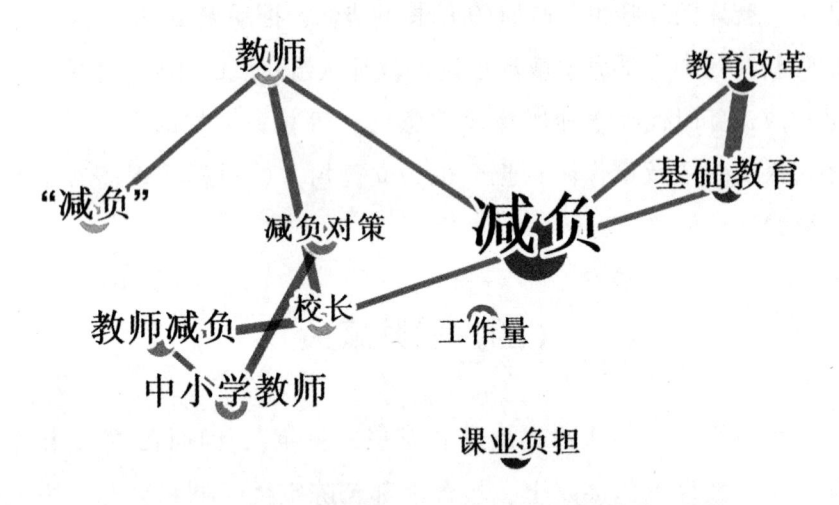

图9　2019年与"教师减负"相关文章的关键词共现网络

（五）教育国际化

教育国际化是教育强国的必然选择。《中国教育现代化2035》的十大战略任务中，第九条明确指出，要开创教育对外开放新格局。而在《加快推进教育现代化实施方案（2018—2022年）》中，十项重点任务第九条也是"推进共建'一带一路'教育行动"。2019年度，有部分教育智库关注到这一热点问题，如上海师范大学国际与比较教育研究院（联合国教师教育中心）以"国际学生评估项目"（PISA）、"教师教学国际调查"（TALIS）为抓手，推动了"中英数学教师交流项目"，并在2019年年底PISA成绩公布时，引发了学术界的热议。在这一基础上，该中心陆续推出了各类教育国际交流的研究报告和学术论文，相关决策咨询报告获得了国家和省部机关的肯定性批示。此外，长江教育研究院在这一问题上也不断拓新，举办的"'一带一路'沿线教育智库对话会"，其成果也获得了教育部相关司局的肯定。

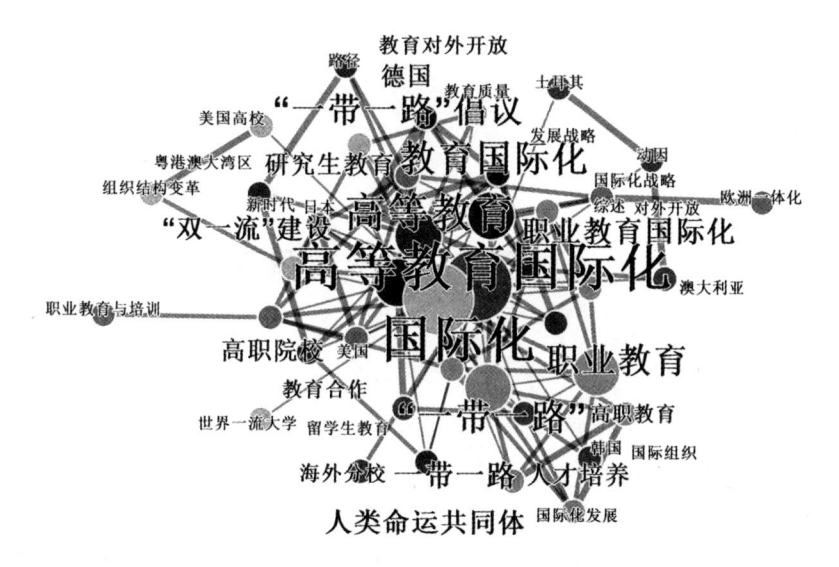

图10　2019年与"教育国际化"相关文章的关键词共现网络

当然，以上仅列举遴选智库关注的主要政策热点问题研究，此外，还有如产教融合、高考改革、学校安全、教育扶贫、家庭教育等问题也是各智库关注的焦点。而对于地方教育智库而言，他们更多地会关注到中央政策在本区域的落实问题，以及区域内的教育热点难点问题。

五　2019年中国教育智库的发展特点

（一）咨政建言愈发有效

2019年对于中国教育有着特殊的意义。为了贯彻全国教育大会精神，各省市相继召开教育大会，部署落实本区域的教育工作，同时《中国教育现代化2035》的发布，也推动着更多的教育智库以更大的热情投入教育政策研究。2019年，针对国家教育的热点难点，以及结合本区域的教育问题，更多的教育智库明确了自身定位，有针对性地提出咨政建言，获得了政府职能部门更多的认可与采纳。

从2019年年初开始，各教育智库相继组织人手在《人民日报》《光明日报》《中国教育报》以及各种专业学术期刊发表《中国教育现代化2035》的解读文章，引发了社会对中国教育现代化的强烈关注，为《中国教育现代化2035》的推进构建了良好的社会舆论基础。两会期间，长江教育研究院、华中师范大学教育治理与智库研究院等教育智库以推进教育治理放管服改革，扩大高校自主办学权等提案，借助两会时机由全国人大代表周洪宇提交议案"深化教育领域'放管服'改革，推进教育治理现代化"，得到了教育部的回复与采纳。教育部在2019年8月22日答复，将会在"推进政府转变教育行政职能,落实和扩大学校办学自主权""营造良好的社会组织参与教育治理的制度环境""教育去行政化、教育家办学""加快完善国家教育标准体系""探索'互联网+教育监管新体制'""优化教育服务环境""加快教育立法进程""克服'五唯'顽瘴痼疾""构筑一体化教育督导体系"[①]九个方面深入教育领域"放管服"改革。这一政策建议也推动了教育部制定了《深化教育领域"放管服"改革2019年度任务清单》,明确了5方面30项改革重点任务、政策举措和责任分工,为教育治理精准化提供了决策依据。在宏观政策研究方面,北京师范大学中国教育与社会发展研究院、华东师范大学国家教育宏观政策研究院、陕西师范大学西部教育研究中心、天津科技大学天津市教育发展研究中心、天津师范大学翔宇基础教育实践研究所、宁波大学海洋教育研究中心、广州大学教育政策研究中心、北京教育科学研究院、江苏教育现代化研究院等教育智库从"四点一线一面"的国家战略出发,对京津冀一体化教育问题、粤港澳大湾区教育问题、长三角一体化教育问题、长江经济带沿线教育合作、"一带一路"沿线国家教育合作交流问题,进行了深入的调研,有关成果也得到了国家和地方政府领导的批示与采纳。上述几个重要教育智库中,北京师范大学中国教育与社会发展研究院全年报送各级党政领导咨询报告被批示采纳达到17份,其中党和国家领导人批示6份。华东师范大学国家教育宏观政策研究院全年共42份咨询报告被中央和市政府相关领导批示和采纳,其中有2份国家领导批示,26份获教育部及上海市领导批示,14份获有关部门采纳,批

[①] 《对十三届全国人大二次会议第4835号建议的回复》,教育部网站,2019年8月22日,http://www.moe.gov.cn/jyb_xxgk/xxgk_jyta/jyta_zfs/201910/t20191025_405223.html。

示率近60%。东北师范大学中国农村教育发展研究院依托学科优势，递交有关部门并获批的咨询报告有13份，其中1份报告获得国家领导人肯定性批示。长江教育研究院全年向有关部门递交决策咨询报告46份，有25份获得肯定性批示，其中党和国家领导人批示10份。而更多的地方教育智库、地方教科院所，在贯彻各地教育大会精神基础上，起草各地教育现代化2035的实施大纲与路线图，为当地教育决策咨询提供研究报告，起到了服务地方社会的重要作用。如湖南省教育科学研究院编写的《教育决策参考》获得国家领导人批示1项，并有多项对策建议被湖南省政府的教育政策文件采纳；江苏省教育现代化研究院受江苏省教育厅委托，承担《江苏教育现代化2035》研制工作，并向省政府和教育厅提交多份咨询报告，获省主要领导肯定性批示1份；天津科技大学天津市教育发展研究中心参与编制"天津教育现代化2035"和"五年实施方案""义务教育均衡发展三年行动方案"等重要文件，在为天津教育咨政建言方面发挥了智库的价值；淮北师范大学安徽高校管理大数据研究中心完成的《安徽省2018年度高等教育满意度调查分析报告》成为安徽省教育厅研判高等教育质量的重要依据，编制的《淮北市乡村振兴战略规划（2018—2022）》已经成为淮北市乡村振兴的主要文件依据；南京市教育科学研究所组织编写的《南京教育现代化2035》文件，为南京教育的未来发展提供了方向和依据；南京晓庄学院南京教育智库通过调研，撰写"南京民办学校发展状况调研报告"，获得南京市财政局批示采纳，为南京民办学校在2019年进行费用调整提供了理论基础和决策依据。

总体而言，2019年以来各教育智库咨政的热点主要集中在贯彻落实全国教育大会精神、各地市教育现代化2035的起草规划与发布、义务教育均衡化的稳步发展、教育法治化的深入推进等热点政策问题。随着智库概念的不断深入，以及各教育智库对智库功能的理解消化，各智库的决策咨询也逐步精准化，有的放矢，即高端教育智库对准国家宏观教育政策问题，区域教育智库更关注政策落地与教育实践，这样也进一步提高了咨政建言的效率。

（二）合作建设愈发多元

2019年以来，教育智库的合作愈发多元。这其中既有智库与智库的合作，还有智库与媒体的合作，还有智库与政府的合作。

媒体特别是新媒体与智库的合作，进一步提升了智库的社会影响力。智库与媒体的合作，可以让"智库研究的传播扩散不再是单向的行为，而是一种'耦合'过程——智库研究内容在各个平台的传播相互影响，并形成互动，从而将研究内容从国内传播扩散"[①]。在这一前沿思想的引领下，多家教育智库架设了与媒体的合作渠道，借助媒体的传播力扩大智库的影响力。在这一方面，《光明日报》做了引领和表率作用。2019年10月，《光明日报》基础教育智库委员会成立，其定位为聚焦中国基础教育政策决策研究与教改实践，关注和追踪教育热点难点问题，及时回应公众对优质教育的期盼；《广州日报》数据与数字化研究院（GDI智库）也与长江教育研究院等20多家教育智库合作，研制发布"应用大学排行榜""高职高专排行榜""民办高等教育发展报告"等产品，并利用媒体优势进一步扩大成果的社会影响力。新媒体的影响力也不容小觑。方略研究院与长江教育研究院在2019年1月签署合作协议，在教育数据搜集、研制报告、提交内参方面合作共建，并利用方略研究院的"一读EDU"公众号推广智库研究成

---

① 朱瑞娟：《新媒体与西方知名智库的传播机制研究——以"一带一路"建设相关研究传播为例》，《现代传播》（中国传媒大学学报）2018年第4期。

果，其中，由长江教育研究院和方略研究院等教育智库共同评选的"改革开放40年教育人物40名入选名单"在公众号上阅读量高达88000多次，被多人次多公众号转载刊发。

2019年教育智库间的合作也愈发活跃。2019年9月，长江教育研究院、天津大学教育学院、陕西师范大学教育学院、北京外国语大学国际教育学院、华中师范大学教育学院、广州大学教育学院、河南大学教育学院、海南师范大学教育科学学院等21家教育智库发起组建了"一带一路"教育智库联盟，旨在助推"一带一路"沿线国家教育合作。这是目前国内最大的教育智库联盟，囊括了国内多所高校、教育研究机构、媒体等，形成了较大的影响力。这其中，长江教育研究院发挥了很重要的组织、策划和协调作用。2019年1月，江苏大学、江苏现代化教育研究院、长江教育研究院三家教育智库联合举办了"镇江·长江教育论坛"，全国人大常委会委员、中国教育学会副会长周洪宇，南京大学党委书记、江苏省政协副主席胡金波，首都师范大学孟繁华校长，江苏大学颜晓红校长，浙江大学眭依凡教授，华东师大阎光才教授等专家学者共同探讨了高水平大学建设问题；3月，人民教育出版社、长江教育研究院联合举办"北京·长江教育论坛"，会上各专家对教育改革发展的新形势做出预判，主办方还在会上发布了《中国教育政策建议书（2019年版）》《中国教育指数（2019年版）》《2019年十大教育关键词》，全国政协常委、副秘书长、民进中央副主席朱永新，全国人大常委、湖北省人大常委会副主任周洪宇等专家学者出席会议并做主旨发言；4月，南京晓庄学院、华中师范大学教育治理与智库研究院、长江教育研究院、中关村互联网创新教育中心举办"中国教育智库建设论坛"，教育部社会科学司副司长谭方正出席会议，会上中国教育科学研究院、上海师范大学国际与比较教育研究院、北京师范大学中国教育与社会发展研究院、南京师范大学道德教育研究所、南京大学高等教育研究与评价中心、长江教育研究院等国内知名智库负责人在会上介绍了各自教育智库的建设经验；6月，宁波大学、长江教育研究院举办的"宁波·长江教育论坛"对长三角一体化进程中教育的作用问题展开讨论；8月，天津大学、天津师范大学与长江教育研究院联合举办"天津·长江教育论坛"，聚焦雄安新区发展战略，为加快建设雄安新区教育改革开放示范区凝智聚力；9月，陕西师范大学、长江教育研究院合作举办了"西安·长江教育论坛"，就教育全球化进程中"一带一路"沿线国家的机遇予以了深度关注；10月，海南师范大学、长江教育研究院主办的"海南·长江教育论坛"立足海南自贸试验区建设的现实需要，海南省人大常委会副主任康耀红等领导专家出席，充分探讨了促进海南教育改革与创新以及提升海南教育国际化水平的发展战略；同月，天津师范大学与长江教育研究院主办的"天津·长江教育论坛"以"雄安新区发展战略和基础教育高质量发展"为主题，对基础教育的发展展开了深入探讨。可以说，智库与智库的合作，是一种双赢的机制。对于高端教育智库而言，是进一步扩大了人力资源队伍，挖掘各地方教育智库的研究潜力；而对于地方教育智库而言，是通过共建获取了报送渠道，因为渠道建设是绝大多数地方教育智库根本无法凭自身力量构建成功的。如在与长江教育研究院的共建过程中，南京晓庄学院南京教育智库在2019年获得国家领导人批示1项，省部级批示1项。从市属高校的智库建设能力来看，这是一种标杆性智库成果，因为即便是高端教育智库，如北京师范大学中国教育与社会发展研究院和华东师范大学国家教育宏观政策研究院在2019年获得国家领导人的批示也分别是6项和2项。由此可见，共建的效果是立竿见影的。未来，这一模式有可能成为教育智库合作建设的重要发展方向。

表15 "一带一路"教育智库联盟发起单位及成员名单（排名不分先后）

序号	名称
1	长江教育研究院
2	方略研究院
3	华中师范大学教育学院
4	华中师范大学教育治理与智库研究院
5	陕西师范大学教育学院
6	北京外国语大学国际教育学院
7	天津大学教育学院
8	天津师范大学教育学院
9	天津科技大学天津市教育发展研究中心
10	内蒙古师范大学教育学院
11	江苏大学教师教育学院
12	南京晓庄学院教育研究院
13	江苏教育现代化研究院
14	宁波大学教师教育学院
15	温州医科大学中国创新创业教育研究院
16	广州大学教育学院
17	河南大学深圳研究院
18	海南师范大学教育科学研究院
19	云南师范大学教育科学与管理学院
20	广西教育学院
21	广州日报数据和数字化研究院教育智库

智库与政府的合作也在加强。2018年年底，在教育部学校规划建设发展中心指导下，中国教育智库网与海南东方市政府合作举办了"第三届中国教育智库年会暨高端教育智库助力自贸区创新发展研讨会"，聚焦探讨海南自贸区教育的创新发展；2019年8月，中国教育三十人论坛与天水市人民政府联合主办首届中国西部教育发展论坛，论坛以"用教育阻断贫困代际传递"为主题，聚焦西部教育发展中的难点、热点问题，推动西部教育改革发展，

为西部地区消除贫困、建设小康社会建言献策,论坛还发布了《中国西部学前教育研究报告》《中国西部基础教育研究报告》。同时,各教育智库接受政府委托项目也在逐步增多,如长江教育研究院、北京师范大学教师教育研究中心等智库接受教育部教师工作司委托,开展《教师法》修订工作;东北师范大学中国农村教育发展研究院接受教育部教师工作司、政策法规司、基础教育司、民族教育司等教育部司局委托课题6项,围绕农村教育政策、师资及民族农村教育现状问题开展调研工作;江苏省教育现代化研究院接受江苏省教育厅委托,对江苏高考综合改革方案进行可行性论证与风险评估,成为江苏省高考改革方案上报中央"深改办"审批的重要组成部分和支撑。

(三)成果报告愈发专业

近一年来,各教育智库发布了多项教育研究报告。2018年年底,北京师范大学中国基础教育质量监测协同创新中心、北京师范大学中国教育与社会发展研究院、北京师范大学儿童家庭教育研究中心和中国教育报家庭教育周刊联合发布了《全国家庭教育状况调查报告(2018)》,报告通过全国性调研,客观呈现了中国家庭教育的现状及突出问题,为家庭教育的科学研究和相关政策规定提供了科学依据。东北师范大学中国农村教育发展研究院2019年1月发布了《中国农村教育发展报告2019》,报告运用国家统计数据和国内调研数据,针对农村教育发展的现状与成就、问题与挑战、应答与展望三个方面,呈现了2018年度中国农村教育的整体概况。南京师范大学道德教育研究所积极主持参与儿童道德发展数据库建设,继2017年发布《中国儿童道德发展报告》后,进一步承担了中央文明办等部门相关儿童道德发展的文件起草规划工作，在未成年人的思想道德建设方面发挥重要的咨询作用。北京师范大学中国教育与社会发展研究院发布了《社会体制蓝皮书：中国社会体制改革报告 NO.7（2019）》，对社会体制改革创新方面进行了深入细致的研究，对 2018 年的改革走向进行分析，提出了相关政策建议。西南大学西南民族教育与心理研究中心在 2019 年 5 月发布《西藏自治区深度贫困县教育脱贫攻坚"一县一策"工作指导方案》，对西藏自治区 6 个地市 15 个深度贫困县教育脱贫攻坚的问题及举措提出了具体的政策建议。南京大学高等教育研究与评价中心在 2019 年年初发布"双一流建设高校本科教育质量百优榜"，成为国内首个以"双一流"高校本科教学质量为研究对象的报告成果。中华教育改进社在 2019 年年初发布《2018 年度中国教育改进报告》，梳理了中国教育改进的不足之处，并提出了相应的对策建议。21 世纪教育研究院在 2019 年 8 月的《中国西部基础教育研究报告》调研了西部地区的教育情况，指出西部农村教育的区域差距逐步拉大成了西部教育发展的新问题；2019 年 12 月，21 世纪教育研究院还发布了《中国教育公益领域发展研究报告（2019）》，梳理了教育公益领域的发展变化，对社会组织参与教育领域作了预判，进一步定位了未来教育领域中社会组织介入的方向。长江教育研究院在 2019 年 3 月两会前发布《中国教育政策建议书（2019 年版）》，提出要深化教育领域"放管服"改革，推进教育治理现代化，同时出版了《中国教育黄皮书》，以"推动教育高质量发展，建设教育强国"为主题，梳理了国内教育热点难点问题，并提出了相应的政策建议。本年度地方教育智库在这方面也有多项报告，如湖南教育科学研究院编印了湖南教育发展蓝皮书、湖南义务教育质量检测报告、湖南高等教育职业教育质量年度报告等；南京晓庄学院南京教育智库出版了《南京教育财政及教育热点年度报告书（2019 年版）》等。

（四）社会影响愈发扩大

近一年来，教育智库的社会影响越来越大，主要体现一是通过媒体参与引导舆论，二是通过举办各类高端论坛宣传智库思想，三是走向国际宣传中国教育。2019年伊始，各教育智库纷纷在《人民日报》《光明日报》《中国教育报》《中国社会科学报》等主流纸媒撰文，探讨《中国教育现代化2035》的实施路径。两会期间及随后一段时间，教育智库的相关专家借助传统媒体、新媒体等路径，发表关于如教育惩戒权、教育放管服、破"五唯"的相关观点，利用传媒扩大思想传播力度，引发社会的广泛关注。中国教育科学研究院利用《教育研究》期刊平台，对有关教育治理、《教育部关于加强新时代教育科学研究工作的意见》等政策文件进行解读分析，从学理上为整个教育智库界解读政策文件提供了范例。部分智库注重新媒体的运用，借助微信公众号广泛传播思想学说，如长江教育研究院等组织发布的"改革开放40年中国教育的典型代表"、中华教育改进社发布的"2018中国教育改进报告"等均有十万左右的阅读量和转发量。

在举办高端论坛传播智库思想方面，除去上述长江教育研究院智库联盟的相关高端论坛之外，2018年年底，北京教育科学研究院举办了第五届"北京教育论坛"，探讨城教融合视角下教育在城市发展中的使命。同年年底，长江教育研究院主办的"教育智库与教育治理50人圆桌论坛"以聚焦"优先发展教育事业，加快教育现代化，建设教育强国"为主题展开研讨交流，助推教育发展。中国教育科学研究院在2019年4月举办了中国教育科学论坛（2019），论坛深入学习贯彻习近平总书记关于教育的重要论述和全国教育大会精神，统筹推进全国教育科研，聚焦《中国教育现代化2035》、立德树人落实机制、教育评价改革等重大问题；同时，中国教育科学研究院旨在将这一论坛办成"引领教育改革创新的'策源地'、服务国家教育决策的'思想库'和教育科研战线协同创新的'大舞台'，使之逐步成为国内一流、世界知名的教育科学论坛"①。华东师范大学国家教育宏观政策研究院也在4月召开了中国教育发展论坛，探讨人口变动与教育资源配置问题。6月，中国教育三十人论坛与中国发展研究基金会等机构合作召开"中国儿童发展论坛"，关注儿童发展问题。同月，中国教育三十人论坛与上海师范大学、联合国教科文组织教师教育中心联合举办了首届"全国教师教育发展论坛"，会议关注了新时代教师队伍建设与发展问题。8月，中国教育三十人论坛又在天水举办中国西部教育发展论坛，关注西部教育问题改革。北京师范大学首都教育经济研究院联合相关机构在8月召开中国民办教育论坛并发布《2019中国民办教育蓝皮书》，会议探讨了新时代民办教育的改革发展之路，尤其是民办教育促进法修订后办学环境变化的应对措施。9月，广东省教育研究院主办的第七届中国南方教育高峰年会召开，会议以贯彻落实《中国教育现代化2035》，围绕粤港澳大湾区的教育发展展开讨论。以上这些教育智库的论坛大多数已经持续举办多届，形成了良好的品牌形象和社会影响。11月，长江教育研究院、华中师范大学教育治理与智库研究院在北京外国语大学举办第四届"教育智库与教育治理50人圆桌论坛"，聚焦教育治理体系和教育治理能力现代化，邀请了教育部有关领导及学界专家共商教育治理大计。同月，湖南省教育科学研究院主办的首届"教育智库·湘江论坛"上，聚焦人工智能与教育变革，教育

---

① 《中国教育科学论坛（2019）在京召开》，2019年4月18日，中国教育科学研究院网站，http：//www.nies.net.cn/gzdt/wyxw/2019 04/t20190418_ 334753.html。

部科技司雷朝滋司长等专家学者就人工智能时代学校治理模式、教师角色、学生学习方式变革等问题开展研讨。12月，中国教育三十年论坛第六届年会以"科技发展与教育变革"为主题在北京举行，顾明远、徐辉、朱永新等专家围绕这一主题开展学术探讨。

在国际影响方面，目前主要是一些高端教育智库在积极开展公关外交活动，扩大中国教育智库的影响力。2019年北京师范大学中国教育与社会发展研究院与英国牛津大学摄政学院全球发展与展望研究院在牛津联合主办"教育与社会治理现代化"第四届研讨会，中英双方70余位专家学者探讨了教育改革与社会发展、产教融合与社会治理等理论与实践问题，会议在海内外产生了广泛影响。上海师范大学国际与比较教育研究院在2019年出访海外40多人次，智库负责人张民选教授于11月赴巴黎参加联合国教科文组织第40届大会，参与研讨联合国二级机构的工作开展情况，同时该中心还在本年度承担了世界银行全球教育实践局、莫斯科国立师范大学、博茨瓦纳教育行政人员高级研修班等多项国际机构、高校及行政人员的来访与培训工作。由于国际与比较教育研究院的"联合国教师教育中心"的身份，其在国际教育舞台的影响力也不断扩大，对于中国教育走向世界，开展公关外交发挥了重要作用。地方教育智库在国际影响方面也有了重要突破。2019年10月，江苏教育现代化研究院与俄罗斯国家教育科学研究院签署合作协议，共同开展"21世纪中俄教育比较与发展趋势展望"研究，在莫斯科举办了两场智库成果发布会及"中俄教育发展战略比较研讨会"，并受俄罗斯国家杜马教育与科学委员会主席邀请，在俄国家杜马大厦召开了中俄发展战略与合作交流研讨会，最终商定今后将轮流在南京、莫斯科举办智库研究成果发布会。

六　中国教育智库高质量发展的问题

党的十九届四中全会审议通过了《中共中央关于坚持和完善中国特色社会主义制度、推进国家治理体系和治理能力现代化若干重大问题的决定》，全会提出到 2035 年要"基本实现国家治理体系和治理能力现代化"。在实现"治理体系和治理能力现代化 2035"和"教育现代化 2035"的共同进程中，作为教育治理体系和软实力组成部分的教育智库将会发挥更为重要的价值和作用。这不仅是中国特色新型智库协调发展的需要，也是国家治理现代化的内在需求。因而，对照国家治理体系和治理能力现代化的宏远目标来看，当下我们教育智库还存在着一些不足，正如习近平总书记所说的，"随着形势发展，智库建设跟不上、不适应的问题也越来越突出"。

（一）认识跟不上问题依然存在

认识跟不上问题存在于两个方面，一是用库者的认识跟不上，二是建库者的认识跟不上。所谓用库者，即政府及教育职能部门。自两办发布《关于加强中国特色新型智库建设的意见》以后，推动教育智库建设成为教育职能部门的一项重要工作，2014 年及随

六 中国教育智库高质量发展的问题

后数年的全国教育工作会议上都明确提出要加强教育智库建设，一时间教育智库的建设成为热潮。各教育科研机构也努力向教育智库转向，特别是一些强调理论研究的教育部人文社科基地，开始自发有序地向问题导向的教育政策研究转向。"教育智库"一词也成为这些研究机构的建设目标，甚至在2019年年底，连中国教育学会这一类学会机构都被上级要求转型为教育智库，教育部陈宝生部长在12月的中国教育学会40周年成立大会上提出，"中国教育学会要努力打造高水平新型教育智库，书写'奋进之笔'，建设'奋进学会'"。

尽管各方不断提倡要建设教育智库，但事实上在项目组的调研过程中，各教育智库的使用效率还是不够的。这里所谓的使用效率，即教育决策部门在政策决策过程中参考教育智库的意见和建议的效率。在本项目的调研过程中发现，绝大多数的教育智库并没有被各级教育行政部门使用起来，根本原因在于各教育智库缺乏有效的咨政建言渠道，这又不得不让很多教育智库重新回到了理论研究的定位上。在2019年，各省市相继召开各省、各地市教育大会，对本地区出台了一系列的教育政策，在这些政策制定过程中，专家学者应当且必须发挥重要的作用和价值，但根据调查走访发现，教育智库的作用并没有充分显现。除去省市教科院所由于独特的行政属性参与了区域的教育政策制定外，高校教育智库几乎很难融入教育决策过程中去。相对来说，高校教育智库因为汇集了更为专业的学者，比起教科院所更关注微观教育研究而言，高校教育智库的研究质量理当更好。当然，这一问题也并非仅仅是教育职能部门的问题，既有部分高校教育智库以传统科研机构的方式开展活动，不懂得宣传营销和主动对接政府相关部门的情况，也有教育部门缺乏购买服务的规章制度，所以他们宁可使用顺手的下属教科院所,也不愿意因为购买高校教育智库服务承担相应责任。

有库不用是认识跟不上的第一个问题,认识跟不上的第二个问题是有库无智,即建库者的认识跟不上,当然这里的"智"讲的是决策研究。一直以来,决策研究与学术研究之间存在隔阂,传统的学术研究者不屑于决策研究,认为其学术含量低。这一观点在教育研究机构向教育智库转型的过程中尤其明显。学术界有一类观点,认为"咨政建言的研制只是涉及政策范围,而政策主要是研究利益的分配问题,而无关思想,因此智库的职能在他们看来主要是研究技术或策略问题"[①]。事实上,智库也是能够产生重要学术思想的,如兰德公司归纳出来的博弈论等重要理论。但在当前这样的环境中,很多教育智库从基本理论研究向决策研究的转变非常困难,一方面是长期教育理论研究形成的路径依赖,另一方面则是对教育智库的定位认识跟不上,直接导致各种保障措施无法落实。当前教育智库的建设发展很大程度上是各教育研究机构为了落实相关文件精神,逐步开始转向政策研究的,所以一部分教育智库的成立及建设并非主动性的。这就造成部分教育智库无法产出有效的智力产品,仅仅有一个教育智库的名头,因而在本次项目组的遴选过程中,剔除了这一类"有库无智"的机构。另外,还有一些教科院所的转型过程依然缓慢,其情形很像当下的一些社科院,"在学术研究上,……比不过高校;在决策研究上,也比不上政府内部的政策研究室"[②],所以尽管一些教科院所顶着"智库"的名头,却拿不出有效的智库产品。

---

① 李清刚、赵敏:《新型教育智库咨政建言受阻的成因与破解策略》,《教育研究与实验》2017 年第 6 期。
② 李刚:《社会科学院系统为何"热衷"搞智库研究与智库评价》,《邓小平研究》2019 年第 1 期。

（二）人才跟不上问题愈加明显

2019年以来，人才跟不上问题已经成为制约教育智库发展的另一大桎梏。人才跟不上问题主要是两个方面，一是各教育智库的专业人才数量明显不足，二是教育智库的研究人员专业水准不足。

就第一点而言，由于教育智库是新兴事物，各单位在这一方面的人才储备是不足的。除去中国教育科学研究院、国家教育发展研究中心等机构具有强大的人才储备外，很多教育智库均在组建初期，极度缺乏专业研究人员。这其中，有些高校教育智库由于能够招聘、招录博士后或博士研究生，从而充实了研究队伍，如北京师范大学中国教育与社会发展研究院、华东师范大学国家教育宏观政策研究院、上海师范大学国际与比较教育研究院，这一类高校教育智库由于建设较早，且由高校领导兼任中心主任，在博士生招生等方面具有一定的指标优势，如华东师范大学国家教育宏观政策研究院单列了"教育决策与政策分析博士生培养专项计划"，培养在读及毕业博士生共计44人，这就完全充实了该智库的人员数量，研究成果也有了质量的保障。但以上所举均系个案，并非所有的教育智库均有人才数量方面的保障，更多的教育智库甚至还在依赖大量的兼职研究人员开展工作。而地方教科院所智库一直关注微观教育研究，强调在课程、教学等方面的引领作用，所以其人才储备方面多以学科教育为主，极为缺乏宏观政策研究方面的人才。而囿于其关注定位，地方教科院所又很少会招聘教育政策方向研究人才，这就导致在政策研究方面无人可用。

第二点问题是教育智库研究人才的专业水准。调研显示，除去部分高端教育智库外，大多数教育智库专业水准不足。在"智库热"的过程中，为了迅速贯彻落实中央及教育部有关文件精神，教科院所及高校开始组织原有的研究机构转型为智库，而其基本班底的研究人员的学术背景依然多为教育基本理论等，这就造成教育政策研究的成果理论性重于实践性，缺乏现实问题导向，无法顺利转化为政府决策。在本项目中，高校教育智库占比达到了66%，而结合多所高校教育智库的调研，我们发现，尽管各机构希望做好决策研究为教育改革做贡献，但现在紧缺的是没有做教育政策研究的人员，不得已抽调教育基本理论研究等方向的人员，而这些研究人员在公共政策决策方面存在先天性知识不足，在定量研究方面缺乏经验，无论是研究方法还是研究结果，都无法满足智库的前瞻性、预测性需求，导致决策研究效果不佳，无法为政府部门所信任。除去现有研究人员转型存在的困难外，相关高校缺乏教育政策专业的人才培养，也造成教育智库人才队伍建设后继乏力，这些都成为教育智库未来发展的阻碍。这一现象在地方教科院所也同样存在，长期以来重视课程教学方面的研究，对区域宏观政策研究方面的人才储备不够，也导致其成果的专业性略显不足。社会教育智库相对而言，由于机制的灵活性，聘请专业人员更加精准高效，效果反而会略好于其他几类教育智库，但另一方面又存在着研究人员黏性不强等其他问题。

总而言之，教育智库专业人才不足、现有人才专业性不强已经成为制约教育智库下一步高质量发展的最主要问题。

（三）管理不适应问题亟待破解

管理不适应问题长期存在，体制机制改革推进迟缓，最主要体现在制度管理依然推进迟缓。虽然国家对高端智库的管理办法已经发布数年，但各地、各高校等对教育智库的制度建设诸如旋转

六 中国教育智库高质量发展的问题

门机制建设、应急制度、经费使用制度方面并无太多机制创新之处，导致部分教育智库囿于现有制度制约发展缓慢。

在旋转门机制建设方面，尽管从两办文件到教育部文件中都提出了制度的推行，特别是2019年10月教育部颁发的《教育部关于加强新时代教育科学研究工作的意见》，再次强调"建立持久良性的'旋转门'机制，促进优秀科研人员到党政机关、事业单位、国有企业等机构任职，聘请有实践经验和科研能力的行政领导、学校校长（教师）、企业高层次人才等到教育科研机构担任专职或兼职研究员"[1]，但现实中少有典型的示范案例。虽然有个别行政人员转至教育智库的案例，如山东省教育厅一级巡视员张志勇"旋转"至北京师范大学中国教育政策研究院，但从智库"旋转"至教育行政部门的案例却非常之少。这一问题归根到底还是管理制度上的不足造成的。虽然教育部出台了鼓励"旋转门"的制度，但具体与省一级政府对接的落实细则并未出台，同时作为与教育部对等的省一级地方政府，是否认同并制定细则也成为未知。另一方面来说，在法律层面，《国家公务员法》的相关规定造成"高校智库从事政策研究的人员进入政府机关的法律依据缺失，阻碍了高校智库人员的'旋转'"[2]，而这一问题如何解决还需要在法律层面进行修订。

在应急制度建设方面，教育智库在应急问题时的快速反应机制明显不足。大多数教育智库由于转型问题，主要还是聚焦于原研究方向，当国家及地方重大教育政策出台时，缺乏参与研究热点问题的能力，不能有效参与重大教育决策问题的研讨，不能在这

---

[1] 《教育部关于加强新时代教育科学研究工作的意见》，2019年11月7日，教育部网站，http://www.moe.gov.cn/srcsite/A02/s7049/201911/t20191107_407332.html。
[2] 李晶、刘晖：《旋转门：高校智库服务政府决策的制度创新》，《教育发展研究》2018年第7期。

一研究领域形成话语权，有效引导研究和舆论进展。而当负面教育舆情出现时，大多数教育智库缺乏与媒体、自媒体合作的基础，无法在舆论引导方面起到良好的效果，如2019年年底南京市开展义务教育学校违规办学行为问题专项整治专项督查行动，由于督查工作理解不准确、执行规定简单化，引发了网上强烈的舆论批评，而当地教育智库却未能就这一问题从政府职能部门的角度发声，缺乏公共危机情况下的应急反应。当然这一问题目前还是一种普遍性现象，亟待各地教育智库从体制机制建设方面着力予以破解，深度参与到各类应急问题中。

经费制度的改革依然没有太大进展。目前，国家高端智库规定劳务费不设上限，但调研显示绝大多数教育智库依然受限于劳务费、咨询费等费用使用规定，部分高校教育智库还坚持科研经费总量中10%为劳务费及专家咨询费的底线，造成无法给本部门临时加班人员或外部门临时聘请人员发放经费。如项目组调研的淮北师范大学安徽省高校管理大数据研究中心依据的《安徽省重点智库专项经费管理办法（试行）》，文件明确规定"项目责任单位在编在岗人员不能发放劳务费"，而该智库很多应急性、临时性的咨询报告都是智库研究人员加班完成，这样的规定扼杀了研究人员的积极性；而10%的劳务费经费总量又迫使该智库无力购买外包服务，长此以往必然会影响智库的有序发展。

（四）传播不适应问题尚需改善

相较于政治、经济智库的传播力而言，教育智库在这一方面还存在很大的改善空间，由于定位不明晰的问题，很多教育智库还没有重视传播力的价值和作用，意识较为淡薄。"智库传播是影响

六 中国教育智库高质量发展的问题

智库发展的重要因素，也是新型智库建设的重要内容"①，在这一方面教育智库有必要加快推进发展。

在传播形象塑造方面，教育智库需要向人大重阳、CCG、盘古智库等政治经济类智库加强学习，向社会大众塑造出良好的传播形象。目前就国内教育智库而言，中国教育科学研究院、国家教育发展研究中心这一类智库，由于受到成果涉密的限制，多强调以内参、专报、快报等形式为党政职能部门服务，对智库传播形象塑造重视不够。而高校教育智库虽然对热点关注迅速，各类传播限制也少，但受制于经费限制，在形象塑造方面也乏善可陈，除去上海师范大学国际与比较教育研究院等少数几家比较重视形象塑造外，大多数高校教育智库还没考虑到这一方面的工作。地方教科院所由于其半官方性质的背景，在这一方面受到的限制也很大。相对而言，社会教育智库在传播形象塑造方面由于不受体制限制相对灵活，所以形象塑造方面相对较好，如长江教育研究院、21世纪教育研究院。

在传播渠道建设方面，体系建设不够全面，很多教育智库还未能够建设起传统媒体与新媒体结合的渠道，如电视、报纸、网站、微信公众号、微博、抖音等，无法扩大智库的受众面，无法提升社会影响力。在传统媒体传播方面，与电视等媒体的关系不够紧密，很多教育智库缺乏曝光度。在网站建设方面，很多教育智库的网站内容常年不更新，甚至一些教育智库还无法查找到网站，如作为国家高端教育智库培育单位的北京师范大学中国教育与社会发展研究院，迄今还未能查到网站，给对外交流传播造成了一定的阻碍。在新媒体传播方面，除微信公众号这一渠道外，微博、

---

① 冯雅、李刚：《新型智库传播现状与优化策略研究——基于CTTI来源智库媒体影响力的实证分析》，《图书与情报》2019年第3期。

抖音以及国际网络社交媒体平台等，少有教育智库注重经营与维护。这一点相较于美国智库而言，差距非常明显。

在传播范围方面，多注重在国内传播，国际传播鲜有成功案例。据2020年1月30日由美国宾夕法尼亚大学"智库研究项目"（TTCSP）发布的《全球智库报告2019》显示，全球顶级智库百强榜单中，中国智库上榜8家，无一教育智库；亚洲大国（中国、印度、日本、韩国）智库百强榜单中中国入选27家，也无一教育智库。这说明中国教育智库的传播力还未能辐射到国际范围，对国际教育治理的影响力有限，未能够引发国际智库研究界的关注。就目前国内智库而言，仅有上海师范大学国际与比较教育研究院由于有"联合国教科文组织教师教育中心"的头衔，能够积极发挥国际交流传播的作用，其他教育智库与西方教育智库的交流少见报道。缺乏有效的国际教育智库交流渠道成了阻碍中国教育智库思想传播，限制发挥公共外交功能的重要因素。

七 中国教育智库高质量发展的建议

教育强国目标的实现既需要脚踏实地的操作实践，也需要高瞻远瞩的顶层设计。为实现《中国教育现代化2035》的宏伟目标，我们需要更多的、更高质量的教育智库群策群力，共同发挥作用和价值。因此，从考虑教育智库高质量发展的角度出发，我们认为今后还需要从以下几点着力加强建设，稳步推进教育智库发展。

（一）进一步提升各方对教育智库的认识

首先，要进一步提升建库者的认识，帮助教育智库明确自身的定位，尤其是要厘清智库与学术研究机构的差别。这里的建库者不仅包括了智库的负责人、建设者，还包括了教育智库的上级分管领导。以高校教育智库为例，尽管智库的实际负责人非常明确其定位与目标，但获取人、财、物的资源却依然还要依靠分管校领导的支持。所以从这个意义上来说，建库者不仅仅包含了教育智库的负责人，也应当包括其上级分管领导。一旦分管领导认识到教育智库的重要性，智库的发展自然也会顺风顺水。因此，我们建议要进一步通过学习、培训等方式帮助"建库者"明确智库的价值和意义，特别是其在教育强国、教育现代化2035、教育治理体系与治理能力现代化中发挥的重要作用。具体可以由教育部社科司牵头，从全国一盘棋的统筹出发，建立"教育智库培训共同体"，邀请影响力较大的教育智库如中国教育科学研究院、国家教育发展研究中心、北京师范大学中国教育与社会发展研究院、长江教育研究院等开设决策研究课程，为国内教育智库负责人开设培训课程。同时还可以聘请国外知名高校智库、科研院所的研究人员，尤其是引介美国教育政策研究联盟、伊利诺伊大学香槟分校国家学习成果评估所、布朗大学安纳伯格学校改革研究所、亚利桑那州立大学全球教育高级研究中心等这一类美国高校教育智库的成功经验，消除国内教育学界关于决策研究和理论研究之间的隔阂，强调凸显智库研究与学科发展一体两面的关系，才能够破解当下诸如高校教育智库、地方科研院所向决策研究转型的困惑。在这一过程中，建议社科司要凸显一些教育部人文重点基地由理论研究向决策与理论并重研究的率先垂范作用。此外，培训课程还要考虑决策咨询的精准性、智库产品的品牌性、服务范围的差异性等多个角度，以帮助各智库特别是高校教育智库和地方教科院所能够因地制宜、因时制宜，产出更多更有效的决策成果。

其次，要进一步提升用库者的认识，特别是教育行政部门对教育智库价值和作用的认识。在这一方面，既需要各级教育行政部门认真学习贯彻落实两办关于智库建设的相关文件，也需要自上而下的学习培训改变认识，更需要教育智库能够提供高质量的决策成果来改变用库者的认识。要使教育决策研究成果让决策者想得到、用得上、离不开，才能彻底改变用库者对教育智库的认识，因而，教育智库的研究成果质量也在一定程度上决定了用库者的认识。智库主动与政府重大发展战略对接，关注教育的前瞻性问题、预警性问题，能够提交高质量的决策报告，才能真正实现"有库有智"。考虑到智库管理协调的特殊性，我们建议各级宣传部门可以根据本地情况，遴选高质量教育智库纳入宣传部统一管理、建设与评估范围，搭建政府与智库沟通的桥梁，在运用、沟通、协调、评价等方面开展整体性的治理，盘活并真正用好所属范围内的教育智库。

（二）进一步加强教育智库人才的培养

高质量的教育决策研究成果产出取决于高质量从事教育政策研究的人员。只有人才培养跟得上，智库的专业人才队伍建设和研究的专业水准才能够得到提高，而人才培养最主要还是要依靠高校的规模化培养。

鉴于当前国内教育学科培养模式的现状，我们建议一是具有教育学硕博士授予权的高校尽快全面推进自主设置教育政策学二级学科，先行将教育学、管理学等学科的教师队伍组合，结合本校本地实际情况开展教育政策学人才培养。有条件的高校可以与北京师范大学、华东师范大学等已有一定培养规模的高校合作，逐步提升本校培养层次，尤其要借鉴学习华东师范大学国家教育宏观政策研究院的"教育决策与政策分析"博士生培养专项计划，该计划2019年招收的10名博士生分别来自教育学、人口学、社会学、人文地理、语言学、城市规划等不同学科，部分高校可以将这一模式复制到本校，先从硕士生专项计划开始推进，逐步扩大范围并提升培养效果。二是在课程设置时要紧密围绕教育政策研究的目标，除去教育学基本理论课程以外，还要不断加强管理类课程的学习，包括公关政策学、政策分析方法、比较教育政策、人口政策、决策定量分析等课程，从而实现培养目标的精准性。有条件的高校可以将管理学与教育学两个学科打通，联合设置课程，开展人才培养。三是一定要加强跨学科研究方法的渗透，特别是定量研究方法的学习掌握，如教育测量与统计、政策评估等，以助于在政策研究中用数据说话。除了对现有人才进行跨学科研究方法的培训外，还可以考虑招收、招聘一些其他专业的人才，如经济学、人口学、管理学、统计学，利用研究人才队伍的专业复合化，推进跨学科研究方法的深化。四是以培养促研究，在人才培养的过程中尽可能推动培养机构成为教育智库，特别是有硕博培养授权单位的教育政策研究机构，要多向北京师范大学中国教育与社会发展研究院、华东师范大学国家教育宏观政策研究院、东北师范大学中国农村教育发展研究院、上海师范大学国际与比较教育研究院等智库学习先进经验，通过人才培养推动政策研究的深入；反过来也要做到以研促培，以现实教育问题的研究推动现有研究人员深入研究，提高研究质量，在这一点上，无法通过招生提升研究队伍的如地方教科院所、普通地方高校可以借鉴长江教育研究院等机构的做法，不断推出系列高质量研究产品，倒逼现有研究人员提升水平。

（三）进一步深化教育智库管理体制机制改革

结合《教育部关于加强新时代教育科学研究工作的意见》要求，进一步深化教育智库管理体制机制改革，特别是在"旋转门"机制建设、应急机制建设、经费制度建设方面推出一些具体的实施细则与成功经验。

在"旋转门"机制建设方面，建议教育部社科司协调推进，由各省市教育厅出台本地教育智库"旋转门"具体实施细则，在人员交流方式、交流时限、交流岗位、薪资待遇等方面予以明确。在此方面，各省市可以学习借鉴上海市教育委员会印发的《加强上海高校新型智库建设的指导意见》中的经验："鼓励高校教师到政府挂职或各类研究机构全职从事咨询研究工作。高校保留3%的编制额度专门用于支持教师流动，教师全职到政府或研究机构等工作且人事聘用关系不变的，可保留其事业编制；探索设立特聘岗位、兼职岗位的年薪制，用于吸引政府、高校、研究机构和企业的优秀咨询研究人员。"推进教育智库"旋转门"机制建设，仅仅还局限在教育条口内部，从行政协调角度来说，各省市教育厅的探索会更有便利性。

在应急机制方面，要引导强化教育智库的快速反应能力，建议各地宣传部门将教育智库研究人员与新闻传媒人员混合培训，既是考虑到条口管理的统一性，也是便于科研人员与媒体人员在出现应急情况引导舆论时，有通畅的发声渠道。此外还要建立健全教育智库考评办法，注重对决策部门提出的"短平快"应急项目的适度倾斜，确保在应急情况时人员的充足性。

在经费制度建设方面，建议各地在贯彻落实中央关于智库建设的文件精神基础上，学习借鉴高端智库经费管理办法，加快制定教育智库经费专项管理办法，要区别于传统科研经费管理办法，在劳务费、咨询费等方面要解禁，充分调动智库研究人员的积极性。适当情况下，建议部分高校教育智库可以先行一步，推进个体的实体化发展，设立独立法人及账户，实现经费使用的自主性。

总而言之，在当前整体管理体制机制改革推进缓慢的情况下，我们建议在教育现代化先行省如江苏省，或选取如南京市等地，成立教育智库体制机制改革特区，在经费改革、智库"旋转门"、应急机制、考评办法等方面开展积极有效的探索，为全国各类智库的体制机制改革发展探索新路。

（四）进一步扩大教育智库传播渠道与范围

各教育智库要采取多种措施手段，不断扩大传播渠道与范围，提升智库的影响力。具体而言，建议各机构一是要重视教育智库的传播形象塑造，打破传统的"酒香不怕巷子深"的观念，要能够对外界塑造起有担当、有作为的智库形象，通过举办高端论坛，与媒体搭建共建平台，在教育热点难点问题上敢于发声等多种手段塑造智库形象，打造智库品牌。二是要重视教育智库的传播渠道搭建，既要注重与传统媒体的合作，借助传统媒体的渠道传播思想，也要注重与新媒体的合作，各教育智库可以与传统电视、报纸媒体合作共建举办高端论坛，发挥双方的各自优势，共同扩大影响，同时也要注重智库自身的网站建设、微信公众号推送、微博发布甚至国际社交媒体平台推送相关信息，建构一套完整的新媒体传播体系。此外，还要注重网络营销，通过营销不断获得市场，利用市场占有率影响社会舆论、决策动态，各教育智库可以借鉴学习美国智库的 CRM 模式，如定期向客户邮箱推送智库活动信息，持续打造智库的品牌会议，举办智库注册会员日等活动，增强智库信息订阅者的黏性，从而将传播渠道多元化。三是要重视教育智库的传播范围扩展，要加强与国际教育组织、智库机构的合作，如经合组织的教育与技能局、世界银行的教育全球发展实践局、布鲁金斯学会等，提前谋划合适的教育议题，通过举办对话、高端论坛等形式，扩大中国教育智库的思想传播范围。

附录1 项目组研究大事记
（2019.1—2019.12）

序列	时间	重大活动	地点
1	2019.1.27	镇江·长江教育论坛	镇江
2	2019.3.3	北京·长江教育论坛	北京
3	2019.3.19	中国教育国际竞争力指数发布会	北京
4	2019.4.27	中国教育智库建设论坛	北京
5	2019.6.1	宁波·长江教育论坛	宁波
6	2019.8.19	上海·长江教育论坛	上海
7	2019.8.25	天津·长江教育论坛	天津
8	2019.9.18	调研国际货币基金组织（IMF）	华盛顿
9	2019.9.20	调研布鲁金斯学会、美国国家公共电台（NPR）	华盛顿
10	2019.9.20	第六届和苑和平节（中国世界和平基金会主办）	北京
11	2019.9.26	调研美国全国广播公司（NBC）	纽约
12	2019.9.27	调研今日美国（USA Today）	纽约
13	2019.9.29	西安·长江教育论坛	西安
14	2019.10.12	海口·长江教育论坛	海口
15	2019.10.26	天津·长江教育论坛	天津
16	2019.11.9	2019教育智库与教育治理50人圆桌论坛	北京
17	2019.12.1	广州·长江教育论坛	广州

附录 2　长江教育研究院（CERI）简介

　　长江教育研究院是在湖北省教育厅的支持下，由华中师范大学和湖北长江出版传媒集团有限公司联合发起，于 2006 年 12 月 16 日成立的教育研究机构。全国人大常委会委员、中国教育学会副会长、中国教育发展战略学会副会长、湖北省人大常委会副主任、华中师范大学教授周洪宇担任院长。

　　长江教育研究院本着"全球视野、中国立场、专业能力、实践导向"的指导思想，"民间立场、建设态度、专业视野"的立院原则，聚集了一批国内外优质教育专家资源，搭建了一个以文化出版企业为依托、联系相关教育专家和教育管理部门的平台，形成了以学术研究为基础、政策研究为重点、出版企业为依托、政府支持和社会参与为支撑，"学、研、产、政、社"优势互补、协同推进的新型体制机制。

　　12 多年来，长江教育研究院一直致力于打造新型教育智库"重器"，努力让智库的"谋划"转化为党和政府的决策，智库的"方案"转化为实际行动，智库的"言论"转化为社会共识，更好地为改革奉献力量。2016 年、2017 年连续两年在中国智库索引评选中社会智库类 MRPA 测评综合排名全国第三，MRPA 资源效能

附录 2 长江教育研究院（CERI）简介 ▶▶▶

测评全国第一。2017 年入选中国社会科学评价研究院 "2017 年度中国核心智库"。2018 年在中国智库索引社会智库类 PAI 值评分榜排名全国第二。

附录3 华中师范大学教育治理与智库研究院（ETTG）简介

华中师范大学教育治理与智库研究院（Research Center for Educational Governance and Think Tank，简称ETTG）是以教育智库、教育智库指数、教育治理为主要研究对象，秉持为政府部门提供教育决策咨询、引导社会舆论、推动建设教育强国为宗旨的教育智库。它由全国人大常委会委员、湖北省人大常委会副主任、中国教育学会副会长、长江教育研究院院长、华中师范大学教授周洪宇领衔，以华中师范大学为依托，与长江教育研究院共建，全面整合两者科研资源与人才队伍，以建设"中国一流高校教育智库"为目标，力争建成在全球教育智库与教育治理领域具有显著影响力和权威性的研究与创新平台、评价与发布中心，充分运用高校与教育科研机构在学术思想、理论上的长处，为政府战略性决策、第三方评估提供可行性方案。

ETTG开展教育智库、教育治理、教育智库指数与评价研究，教育调查及教育政策研究，定期公布全国教育智库排名情况，为我国教育智库发展提供科学的评价数据；每年定期举办"教育智库与教育治理50人圆桌论坛"，召集全国教育及其他相关领域知名专家对重大教育问题进行研讨交流；还将着力研究世界知名教

附录3 华中师范大学教育治理与智库研究院（ETTG）简介

育智库的运行机制、特点，积极参与全球智库交流活动，逐步扩大中国教育智库在国际上的知名度和影响力。中心致力于推动我国教育智库建设与教育治理改革，提升中国教育智库的国际知名度与话语权。

教育智库与教育治理50人圆桌论坛（China Educational Think Tank and Governance 50 Forum，简称CETTG50）成立于2017年12月16日，是中国最具影响力的非官方、非营利性教育智库平台之一，专注于教育领域的智库、政策研究与交流，以此推动具有中国特色的新型教育智库建设，全面推进中国教育领域的综合改革，促进教育治理体系与治理能力现代化。CETTG50正式成员由40余位教育精锐组成，未来根据需要将考虑吸收一些教育行业之外的经济学家、企业家、政界领袖成为论坛核心成员，产生更多的思想碰撞。CETTG50于每年11月举办，规模也将逐步扩大，力争打造成为著名论坛品牌。教育智库与教育治理50人圆桌论坛已成功举办两届，在教育界及智库界产生了广泛影响。

中心研究人员在重要期刊发表论文100多篇，出版著作20多部，在各类媒体发表评论200多篇，并广泛参与政府部门各类教育政策咨询活动。中心已与长江教育研究院、南京晓庄学院、广州大学、陕西师范大学、天津科技大学等单位合作成功举办了多次论坛、活动。

附录4　建设好社会智库　助推国家治理现代化

近些年，社会智库雨后春笋般蓬勃发展。一批知名社会智库在理论研究、咨政建言、社会服务、国际交流等方面发挥了重要作用，如全球化智库、中国丝路智谷研究院、盘古智库、海国图智研究院、中国经济改革研究基金会、察哈尔学会、长江教育研究院等均十分活跃。上海社会科学院智库研究中心发布的《2018中国智库报告》显示，社会智库有57家，占智库总数的11.2%。社会智库已成为中国智库体系的重要组成部分。2019年1月31日，美国宾夕法尼亚大学"智库研究项目"（TTCSP）发布《全球智库报告2018》，1家中国社会智库再次进入"2018全球顶级智库百强榜单"。可见，中国社会智库已经在全球智库界崭露头角，初露锋芒。在中国多元化智库主体格局中，社会智库作为民间智慧、思想的代表，必将在国家的决策咨询体系及公共外交中发挥越来越独特而重要的作用。这不仅是中国特色新型智库协调发展的需要，更是国家治理现代化的内在需求。

助推改革开放与国家治理现代化

过去一段时间，社会智库对完善中国特色新型智库体系、促进党和政府科学民主依法决策、深化国家改革开放、推动国家治理体系和治理能力现代化、提升国家软实力做出了实实在在的贡献，成为国家治理现代化的助推器。当前，以数字化、网络化、智能化为主要特征的全球第四次工业革命不期而至，它将深刻改变人与人、人与物、物与物之间的固有关系，对人类社会产生巨大冲击，同时也带来新的发展机遇。国内经济社会转型任务重、人民日益增长的美好生活需要和不平衡不充分的发展之间的矛盾突出；国际上全球化浪潮迅猛、民粹主义抬头，贸易争端、经济动荡、数字鸿沟、气候变化等传统与非传统的全球问题，都对中国的改革开放和国家治理提出了更高的要求。在此过程中，作为连接决策者和社会、公民的特殊力量，社会智库应有紧迫感、使命感，聚焦我国发展面临的突出矛盾和问题，深入调查研究，为化解中国改革开放和国家治理面临的挑战出谋划策，提供高质量的研究咨询成果。

主动与国家战略需求对接是社会智库长远发展的基础。登高方能望远，社会智库要想谋求长远发展，需具备家国情怀与全球视野，把自身成长与国家战略需求紧密结合起来。在中国推动经济社会高质量发展、扩大改革开放、积极参与全球治理、推进"一带一路"倡议的宏观背景下，社会智库应积极与国家战略需求对接，以问题和目标为导向，为国家提供具备战略前瞻、风险预警功能的政策产品，满足国家发展需求。社会智库在对内提供建设方案，对外发出中国声音，化解国际社会对"一带一路"倡议的质疑、观望乃至阻碍，构建人类命运共同体的理论与实践等方面，均大有可为。

保持资金来源多元化

　　智库具有非营利性和客观性的特征。非营利性即公益性，是世界各国智库的基本定位。客观性要求智库独立自主开展研究咨询工作。我国的社会智库应在坚持为党和政府服务的大前提下，坚持非营性利和客观性；秉持民间立场、建设态度、专业精神、实践导向；开展科学研究进而形成专业判断，不奉迎行政部门或利益集团；坚持开展基于证据和实证的研究，用事实、数据说话，保证政策研究与咨询的客观真实。

　　社会智库正常运行需要充足的资金作为保障，资金来源多元化是社会智库保持客观性的重要前提。多元化的资金来源，可以保障社会智库的产品的客观性和科学性，而非为利益集团代言，盲目附和，缺乏基本立场。当前，我国社会智库不乏资金支持，但资金来源仍是困扰社会智库发展的一个重要因素。由于中国的智库产品市场尚未发育成熟，缺乏规范的智库产品供给体系，资金来源渠道单一、缺乏透明度，社会捐赠制度及文化滞后等，成为影响社会智库竞争力和公信力的一个障碍。《关于社会智库健康发展的若干意见》虽明确提出"拓宽社会智库筹资渠道，构建多元化、多渠道、多层次的社会智库资金保障体系"，但具体落实措施尚未具体化。相关部门可尽快着手研究制定针对社会智库资金来源的支持管理办法，包括完善社会智库设立准入门槛，健全智库产品市场供求体系，完善政府购买智库服务机制，完善公益捐赠及扣税制度，鼓励企事业单位、社会组织、基金会、个人捐赠资助社会智库建设，并配套相应的激励措施和荣誉制度等。系统化的社会智库资金来源支持，可以最大限度保证社会智库的公益性、客观性，这也是确保社会智库为国家改革开放和治理现代化提供有效智力支撑的重要前提。

搭建政府与民间沟通桥梁

"兼听则明，偏信则暗。"社会智库作为决策咨询的民间力量，为国家科学民主决策选择开启了另一扇窗。决策者只有善于吸纳各方面的真知灼见，才能明辨是非，促使决策更客观、更接地气。搭建政府与民间沟通的桥梁是社会智库的责任担当。《关于社会智库健康发展的若干意见》指出，社会智库应服务科学决策，承担社会责任。坚持将社会责任放在首位，始终以维护国家利益和人民利益为根本出发点，自觉践行社会主义核心价值观，紧紧围绕党和政府决策需要的重要课题，开展咨询研究。

社会智库来自民间，立足基层，具有搭建民众、社会与政府沟通桥梁的独特优势，能把民众的需求与国家发展进行有效对接。为此，社会智库应扎根民间，深入实际、深入一线，倾听百姓呼声，掌握真实情况，以充分的调查研究、数据资料为依据，拿出可操作的、切实管用的咨政建言成果或方案。社会智库应成为衔接理论专业知识与政策实践的桥梁，融合经济、政治、社会、教育、科学、文化、卫生、环境等领域的催化剂，连通国内与全球治理理论及实践的纽带，真正成为改革开放与国家治理现代化的助推器。在对外交往层面，社会智库作为非官方组织，可以成为国家外交的一支重要力量，代表来自中国民间的声音，在国际舞台上表达中国立场、中国主张、中国智慧，争取国际话语权，配合国家达成战略目标。

（作者周洪宇、付睿，原文刊发于 2019 年 7 月 22 日《中国社会科学报》）

附录5 教育智库如何做好公共外交

党中央、国务院近年来在多个文件中明确提出智库要发挥外交功能，并将其列为智库的五大功能之一。习近平总书记多次强调，要"打造智库交流合作网络"，推进"智库外交"。在落实中央这一指导精神的基础上，一些重要的政治、经济、军事智库开始逐步在国际事务中发挥重要作用。在这一点上，教育智库还有较大的空间可以作为。

《中国教育现代化2035》中明确提出"开创教育对外开放新格局"的战略任务，提出要"积极参与全球教育治理，深度参与国际教育规则、标准、评价体系的研究制定"。这一战略任务目标与智库的外交功能高度契合。在未来，教育智库在公共外交中将会有很大的发挥空间，它是讲好中国教育故事、凝聚国人教育自信、传播中国教育文化、推动构建人类命运共同体的重要渠道之一。

《中国教育智库评价SFAI研究报告（2019年版）》明确提出，国际影响力指标应涵盖国际合作、国际推广、聘请海外员工等指标选项。这既是对国内教育智库外交功能的一次审视，也是一种督促，更是为了快速推进教育智库外交功能的发展建议。在当下教育智库的建设发展中，各类教育智库在国际影响力上还有所欠缺，如在国际教育事务的参与、国际教育机构人员构成、国际教育机构合作、共建、推广等事务上都存在种种不足,这与我们推进教育现代化、建设教育强国的目标是不吻合的,需要不断改善。

当前及今后一段时期内,我们要合理聚焦教育智库外交的范围,抓住重点、稳步辐射,不仅要抓住落实教育部《推进共建"一带一路"教育行动》文件的机遇,将教育智库外交的重点放在"一带一路"沿线国家,对接沿线国家的教育需求,形成经贸合作与教育发展双轮驱动之势,而且要努力扩大教育智库外交的辐射范围,通过相互交流合作,将中国教育的经验和理念传播到世界各国。教育智库界为此应着眼于以下三点工作:

一是进一步加强与国际教育组织的合作。目前我国的教育智库实现国际共建的有四家单位,即北京师范大学、上海师范大学、南方科技大学、海南省教育研究培训院分别与联合国教科文组织共建的国际农村教育研究与培训中心、教师教育中心、高等教育创新中心和联系学校国际中心。对照《中国教育现代化2035》中"深度参与国际教育规则、标准、评价体系的研究制定"的目标,四家合作机构的数量还是不够的。今后,我们不仅要进一步加强与联合国教科文组织的合作,并共建相关教育机构,还要加强与经济合作与发展组织(OECD,以下简称"经合组织")、世界银行等综合性国际机构中教育部门的合作,如经合组织的教育与技能局、世界银行的教育全球发展实践局等,不断扩大中国教育智库与世界顶级机构的合作范围,吸引这些国际重要教育组织与国内高校、教科院所共建智库平台,逐步引导国内教育智库参与国际教育事务的规则、标准制定工作。同时,我们还要借助这些机构在全球的影响力和辐射力,借船出海,不仅要将他们"引进来",还要在全球范围内借助他们的渠道,在其他国家共建教育智库,扩大研究范围,增强中国教育智库的影响力。

二是进一步加强全球范围的教育推广力度。向世界推广中国教育经验，体现的是我们的文化自信及综合软实力。因而，我们要注重古今结合。首先，总结推广中国历史上的成功教育经验与方法，尤其是对发展中国家具有借鉴意义的教育实践路径。如教育家陶行知的生活教育理论，其内核"生活即教育""社会即学校""教学做合一""小先生制"，迄今依然可以成为教育欠发达国家和地区迅速提升教育质量的重要抓手。我们完全可以借助教育智库外交，将生活教育理论引介到"一带一路"沿线国家和地区，既可以帮助他们在短时间内提升教育质量，也可以向世界宣传中国的教育名家与教育思想。其次，提炼当前中国教育改革中的亮点和经验，向全球各国推广，特别是改革开放40年来我国教育战线涌现出的优秀育人模式和方法。例如，上海学生在经合组织的国际学生评估（PISA）测试中体现出的良好素养，就吸引了来自英国等发达国家教育代表团的交流学习，也促成了英文版《真正上海数学》教材的全球首发。这些教育改革中的成功经验与方法也蕴含着我们可以向世界展示的中国先进教育文化。简言之，通过古今结合，可以长时段地展示中国教育的传承与发展、优势与特长，有利于中国教育经验的全球传播。

三是进一步加强国际教育智库人才的培养与交流。据统计，2018年在联合国系统任职的中国籍员工为450人，仅占联合国人员总数的1.09%。在联合国教科文组织中，我国分摊了5.1%的会费，聘用的中国籍员工仅仅占比1.6%。世界银行等国际机构的中国籍员工数量也在2%以下。如果缺乏足够的中国籍员工在世界重要组织中的教育机构任职，那我们想要参与全球教育治理的目标就很难实现。因此，当前及今后很长一段时间内，我们首先要加大国际组织人才的培养。特别是针对联合国教科文组织、经合组织、世界银行等具有教育智库性质的机构，适当在部分高校开设语言、教育等相关课程，甚至设置国际组织人才培养学院，培育一批全球视野与中国情怀相结合的国际教育机构工作人员，建立渠道输送他们进入相关国际教育组织，为中国参与全球教育治理奠定人力资本基础。其次要加强教育智库人才的国际交流。建议由教育部、人社部相关国际交流司局遴选一些高端教育智库中具有良好语言功底的教育政策、教育智库研究者，派驻联合国教科文组织、经合组织教育与技能局、世界银行教育全球发展实践局等机构，了解并参与国际教育标准、规则的制定，同时也积极邀请相关国际组织中的教育学者来华讲学，指导教育政策、教育智库的研究，在不断交流中共同推进人才培养。

  2019年4月26日，习近平总书记在第二届"一带一路"国际合作高峰论坛开幕式的演讲中指出，未来5年，中国将邀请共建"一带一路"国家的政党、智库、民间组织等1万名代表来华交流，共建"一带一路"国际智库合作委员会。这意味着，在未来5年，中国智库的公共外交功能将会发挥极为重要的作用。其中，教育智库也将会有更大的作为空间。因此，作为教育智库的研究者与践行者，我们应当抓住机遇，在人才培养、交流机制、国际共建、全球推广、创设国际教育期刊等方面作出更多努力，推动构建中国教育对外开放的新格局。

（作者刘大伟，原文刊发于2019年12月5日《中国教育报》）

后　　记

　　这是我们连续在中国社会科学出版社出版的第二部中国教育智库评价报告。本来是没有写后记这一打算的，但今年情况特殊，有必要留点历史记忆。由于新型冠状病毒肆虐，我们的团队几乎全部困在武汉，无法动弹。本书的重要作者，我的导师周洪宇教授，这段时间奋战在抗疫第一线，组织湖北省人大常委会教科文卫委员会以及湖北民进的同志们，开设网上医卫、法律、教育、心理等平台为大众服务，接受安排各地民进捐献的医疗物资，作为学生，实在是不忍心打扰他。在疫情最为严重的时候，我跟汉口的师兄视频十分钟，就看到有四辆救护车开进他的小区，所以，我很感激、钦佩本报告的所有参与人，我的老师、我的团队，他们在异常困难的情况下，帮助我一起完成了这部报告。这也是留给我们所有人的集体记忆。2019年年底，我们以为会很快完成报告出版，举办国内与国外的新书发布会，今年的全国调研，等等，看来这一切都只能按下暂停键了。但正如习近平总书记所说的："武汉是英雄的城市，湖北人民、武汉人民是英雄的人民，历史上从来没有被艰难险阻压垮过，只要同志们同心协力、英勇奋斗、共克时艰，我们一定能取得疫情防控斗争的全面胜利。"

后　记 ▶▶▶

祝福武汉！待到春暖花开时，我一定回去看您！

刘大伟

2020 年 3 月 4 日

写在武汉封城第四十二日

China Education Think Tank Evaluation Report

(2020 Edition)

Chapter 1　Background of the Project

Education is the national plan and the CPC's plan. The year 2019 marks the 70th anniversary of the founding of the People's Republic of China. It is also a key year for building a well-off society in an all-round way and achieving the first century-long goal. At the same time, 2019 is the beginning of the full implementation of the spirit of the National Education Conference, and the foundation year for accelerating the modernization of education by 2035 and building a strong nation of education. From the beginning of 2019, the Ministry of Education and various provinces and cities have successively held national education work conferences and education conferences in various provinces and cities to implement and promote the instructions of President Xi Jinping on education at the National Education Conference. At the end of October 2019, the Fourth Plenary Session of the 19th CPC Central Committee reviewed and approved the *CPC Central Committee's Decision on Adhering to and Improving the Socialist System with Chinese Characteristics, Promoting the National Governance System and the Modernization of Governance Capabilities, and Several Important Issues*. One of the most important messages was to " improve the socialist system with Chinese characteristics and promote the modernization of national governance system and governance capacity". As part of the modernization of national governance, one of the important boosters of the modernization of educational governance is the education think tank. Education think tanks have made tangible contributions to improve the new think tank system with Chinese characteristics, promote the scientific and democratic decision-making of the party and government, deepen the country's reform and opening up, and improve the country's soft power. In this historical context, education think tanks from all sides have begun to actively integrate into the national development strategy, transform the deployment of educational power into practical actions, and continue to promote the modernization of education governance system and governance capabilities. Among them, there are not only high-end education think tanks that connect with the "four points, one line, one side" of national macro strategic research, but also local education think tanks that take the development of local education as the research goal and promote the integration of regional education development and society. The education think tanks offer suggestions to build a strong nation of education and provide strong intellectual security. In order to better promote the healthy and orderly development of various types of education think tanks, and to achieve the goal of evaluation and construction, so as to provide more intellectual support for the realization of China's educational modernization 2035, the project team continues to advance the research report on the evaluation of Chinese education think tanks. This report is the second in the annual series of *China Education Think Tank Evaluation SFAI Research Report*. The project team collects and organizes the basic situation of domestic education think tanks by constructing a database of

Chinese education think tanks, researches and judges the problems existing in the development of Chinese education think tanks, finds ways and methods to solve the problems, and supplements them with the evaluation of the education think tanks in the database on various aspects such as structure, function, outcome and influence. The project team hopes to continuously improve the basic data of the domestic education think tank database and eventually become the data analysis center of the Chinese education think tank.

On November 10, 2018, the project team released *China Education Think Tank Evaluation SFAI Research Report* (2018) for the first time in Beijing. The research report summarized the various work each education think tank has done since 2013 based on the important discussion of President Xi Jinping on think tanks. It also sorted out the problems existing in the construction of China's education think tanks and put forward corresponding countermeasures. At the same time, it analyzed the education think tanks in the database, and selected a group of core think tanks with good results and influence. This endeavor received great responses from the education think tank community. Institutes of the education think tanks selected into the database published many news reports, which constituted positive social reaction and built a good interactional mechanism of "evaluation-construction" among different think tanks. They were normal university education think tanks such as Northeast Normal University Research Institute of Rural Education, Center for Studies of Education and Psychology of Ethic Minorities In Southwest China of Southwest University, Nanjing Normal University Institute of Moral Education and so on, comprehensive university education think tanks such as the Higher Education Research and

Evaluation Center of Nanjing University and the Marine Education Research Center of Ningbo University, and internationally-constructed education think tanks such as the Shanghai Normal University's Institute of International and Comparative Education, Nanjing Institute of Educational Science and other local educational research institutes. Moreover, they also included local college education think tanks such as Huaibei Normal University Anhui Big-Data Research Center on University Management, Jiangsu University Education Policy Research Institute, Tianjin University of Science and Technology Tianjin Education Development Research Center, Tangshan Beijing-Tianjin-Hebei Higher Education Development Research Center, Dongguan Institute of Technology Higher Education Research Institute among others. Their positive comments on the evaluation reports has become an internal driving force for further research on this project.

On April 27, 2019, after continuous revision and improvement, *China Education Think Tank Evaluation SFAI Research Report* (2019) with English translation was published by China Social Sciences Press. Meanwhile, a press conference on the newly published book, which was also the First Forum on Chinese Education Think Tank Construction, was held in Beijing. The conference had representatives from the Department of Social Sciences of the Ministry of Education, and from a range of think tanks including the National Institute of Education Sciences, the China Institute of Education and Social Development of Beijing Normal University, the United Nations Teacher Education Center of Shanghai Normal University, the Research Institute of Educational Governance and Think Tanks of Central China Normal University, Nanjing Normal University Institute of Moral Education, Nanjing University Higher

Education Research and Evaluation Center, Yangtze River Education Research Institute and other important education think tanks. They joined the gathering and gave lectures on relevant topics. After the conference, the project team further adjusted and improved the indicator system, surveyed and visited various education think tanks, collected and sorted information and data with the aid of the CETTE (China Education Think Tank Evaluation) platform. Then we analyzed the data through both subjective and objective evaluation methods and combined our analysis with the opinions of experts in this field. With all these efforts, we finally finished this year's *China Education Think Tank Evaluation Research Report*.

Chapter 2 Purposes, Principles and Methods of the Project

To achieve the goal of "constructing and improving the modern education decision-making service system", the project team hopes to play a role of "promoting construction with evaluation" in a reasonable and effective way through the combination of evaluation and construction, and comprehensively promote the sound development of education think tanks.

(1) Clarify the purpose of education think tank evaluation

In the final analysis, the purpose of education think tank evaluation is to help realize the modernization of education in China. *China Education Modernization* 2035 puts forward the overall goal of "to modernize education by 2035, to enter the ranks of a strong country in education, and to promote our country to become a country of great learning, a strong human resource, and a strong country of talent" and plans ten strategic tasks to be done. The role of education think tanks is very important to achieve the overall goals and implement the top ten tasks. Education think tanks can not only gather and educate talents to achieve the goal of strengthening the country with talents, but also provide specific grasps and implementation paths for the implementation of each major task by constructing a modern education decision-making service system. Therefore, from the realization of China's education modernization 2035 goal plan, we must use evaluation to summarize the experience of the construction of education think tanks, find problems in the construction of education think tanks, and explore ways and paths to solve the problems, instead of creating false prosperity of education think tanks with simple evaluation rankings.

From this perspective, the purpose of the education think tank evaluation system is to select a group of typical excellent education think tanks, summarize their development experience, and jointly discuss and solve problems in development, and transfer their experience to help establish more better education think tanks, providing comprehensive support for the realization of the goal of education modernization 2035 in macro decision-making and front-line practice.

(2) Establishing principles of education think tank evaluation

First, adhere to the principle of unity of theory and practice. Compared with other think tanks, education think tanks still have some special characteristics. It is not only "top of the sky", it must take into account the macro layout of educational decision-making; it must also "stand on the ground", it must be combined with the actual education and teaching situation of major, middle and primary schools. Therefore, the evaluation of an education think tank is not only to see how much this think tank has played in advising and advising on politics, but also to consider its practical value for the practice of China's first-line education reform. the project team always follows the principle of combining theory with practice, and fully considers education think tanks that are committed to grass-roots education practice and exert a significant influence and role, such as various educational institutions of all levels. In fact, the practice of grass-roots educational institutions and their impact on the local education administration are often ignored by some comprehensive think tank evaluation lists.

Second, adhere to the principle of unity of content and form. President Xi Jinping has criticized some think tanks for "much form communication and little content innovation" and "formalist practices such as building platforms, inviting celebrities, and setting up forums", so when we evaluate education think tanks, we closely follow the instructions of President Xi Jinping and adhere to the principle of unity of content and form, paying attention to both the influence of education think tanks and the content construction of education think tanks. We always adhere to the "structure-function" theory, and in addition to examining the functions of "resulting power" and "influence" produced by education think tanks, we also focus on the structure of education think tanks, such as the overall framework of education think tanks and daily activities. We not only pay attention to the substantive development process of education think tanks, but also focus on the research quality and content innovation of its results, and its goal is to completely prevent "empty think tanks" from being among the list of the selected education think tanks.

Third, adhere to the principle of strict selection and encouragement of development. The construction and development of education think tanks is a process of steady progress. In 2016, Hao Ping, the then Deputy Minister of Education, pointed out at the National Education Research Institute working conference that "the next 5 years will be a golden period to highlight the role of education and scientific research and to make education think tanks bigger and stronger". [1] In the past four years, the number of education think tanks has been increasing, but with the goal of building an educational power, there is still a large gap between the number and quality of education think tanks and future needs. Therefore, in the evaluation process, the project team insisted on the combination of strict selection and encouragement of development, and eliminated some so-called "education think tanks" that are not deserved. We also selected some education think tanks which are just beginning to develop, especially those in the poor and remote areas. The project team believes that by cultivating, encouraging and developing these education think tanks, they will be more active in policy research and provide more accurate decision-making consultations to solve the problem of imbalances and insufficiency in Chinese education development.

Fourth, adhere to the principle of uniting China and the global perspective. One of the five functions of think tanks is the function of "think tank diplomacy". President Xi Jinping has repeatedly emphasized the role and value of think tank diplomacy. Therefore, in the evaluation process of education think tanks, we must adhere to the unification of

---

[1] *Chinese Education Daily*, Jan. 15, 2016.

China and the global perspective, and based on a deep understanding of China's local education, encourage education think tanks to actively participate in international peer communications and to take specific measures to co-build international institutions, promote international cooperation and recruit overseas employees. Only by telling Chinese education story on the international stage, participating in the discussion of international education topics, and gradually mastering the right to speak the world's education, can China fully demonstrate its educational confidence. Therefore, the project team, as always, pays attention to the "international co-construction" type of education think tanks, which will be the pioneers in telling the Chinese education story to the international education community.

(3) Using scientific methods of education think tank evaluation

At the National Education Conference, President Xi Jinping emphasized that "reversing the unscientific orientation of educational evaluation, resolutely overcoming the stubborn diseases of score-only, progression-only, diploma-only, dissertation-only, hat-only, and fundamentally solve the problem of education evaluation baton"[①]. Therefore, the project team takes the "five-mindedness" as its purpose, builds a "China Education Think Tank Evaluation" (CETTE), uses crawler technology to collect relevant information on the selection of think tanks, and analyzes and selects think tanks through objective data aggregation. We combined field research and

---

① *People's Daily*, September 11, 2018.

the subjective evaluation of experts in the industry, using both subjective and objective evaluation methods to describe the current status of the development of Chinese education think tanks.

Chapter 3 China Education Think Tank Evaluation and 2019 Rankings

(1) Indicators of evaluation

In the process of data collection for *China Education Think Tank Evaluation SFAI Research Report* (2019), we found that (1) education think tanks are generally in the initial development stage. Compared with the maturity of other economic think tanks and political think tanks, education think tanks are obviously not perfect in terms of organizational structure and input guarantee. (2) The vast majority of education think tanks are not substantive operations, so they rely on the parent institution in terms of funding input and system construction. (3) The daily work of many education think tanks mostly overlaps with the parent institution, and it is difficult to distinguish the difference between the two. (4) Some self-reported data cannot be verified for authenticity, which makes it difficult for third-party evaluation.

For all these reasons, the project team has to improve data collection methods and adjust part of the indicator system to keep indicators that are easier to collect data. After adjusting the indicators, we adopt the analytic hierarchy process and Delphi method to recalculate the weight of each indicator, as in the previous study. At the same time, we also added a reference indicator, that is, the time when the think tank was established. The duration of the think tank's existence also has a certain impact on the activity, influence and results of the think tank.

Table 3 – 1　The indicator system of Chinese education think tank evaluation

First level	Second level	Third level
Structure indicators	Organizational structure	Council
		Chief experts
	Institutional guarantee	Funding
		Researchers
		Institutional mechanism
Functional indicators	Think tank daily work	Field visits
		Publication
		New media updates
	Think tank activity	Conferences
		High-end forums
Achievement indicators	Advisory achievement	Internal reports submission
		Advisory reports submission
	Academic achievement	Research papers
		Books
		Research projects
	Application achievement	Educational service
Impact indicators	Advisory influence	Instruction of leaders
		Accepted suggestions
		Plan drafting
	Social influence	Media coverage
		National cooperation
		Research results impact
	International influence	Overseas staff members
		International cooperation
		International communication

Table Continued

First level	Second level	Third level
Development indicator (reference indicator)	Founding time	Founding time

(2) Procedures of evaluation

1. Improving education think tank candidates database

Starting from May 2019, the project team referred to database of the *AMI Research Report on Comprehensive Evaluation of Chinese Think Tanks* (2017) *issued by* Chinese Academy of Social Sciences, the *Chinese education think tank Report 2018: Impact Ranking and Policy Recommendations* issued by the Shanghai Academy of Social Sciences, CTTI of Nanjing University Data platform, *China Think Tank Directory* 2016 and other institutions. We also searched for education think tanks with high levels of activity in various provinces and cities as well as college education think tanks in the central and western regions and nationwide educational institutions. After repeated discussions among the project team members, the number of candidate think tanks for this year's evaluation was increased to 103.

2. Field visits to some education think tanks

This work has begun in early 2019 with a time span of the entire year. The project team conducted research visits to think tanks selected in the previous year and relevant think tanks that entered the candidate pool in the form of field surveys and interviews. Due to the limited staff of the project team, we visited a total of 23 research think tanks related to education throughout the year, both in the form of intensive interviews during meetings and on-site surveys at various think tanks. In fact, in the field survey of think tanks, the project team found out that the online filling and questionnaire reporting adopted by other think tank evaluation systems have produced unreliable data. In view of the small volume of overall education think tank evaluation, the project team intends to further promote field research and strive to run through the selected education think tanks in 2020.

3. Selection operations

From August to October 2019, the project team modified and improved the original CETTE platform, simplifying the input process. At the same time, a maintenance team was formed by the teachers of the School of Information Engineering of Nanjing Xiaozhuang University, and the web crawler technology was used to collect the relevant information of each education think tank in 2019. This includes news reports from various education think tanks on relevant websites at home and abroad, as well as journal article publications and citations of think tanks on CNKI, as well as topics published by the National Philosophy and Social Affairs Office, the National Education Science Planning Office and other websites Quantity, etc. In the end, the project team manually selected the data of each think tank, put them into the CETTE database, and calculated the weighted score. Subsequently, the project team combined data and used multiple rounds of subjective evaluation methods to combine subjective and objective evaluations to score and rank China's active education think tanks.

4. Publishing and further revision

On November 9, 2019, the project team released a simplified version of the "China Education Think Tank Evaluation Report (2019)"

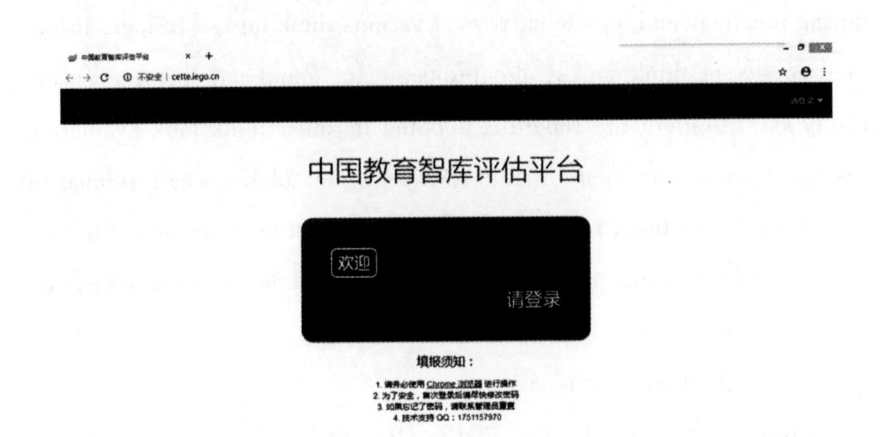

Figure 3 – 1   The Login window of China Education Think Tank Evaluation

at the "2019 Education Think Tank and Education Governance Roundtable Forum" hosted by Beijing Foreign Studies University, and achieved good social response. At the same time, after the meeting, the project team further collected specific information on relevant education think tanks through telephone surveys and field visits based on feedback from various parties, and constantly improved the database to select various think tank data.

5. Experts' evaluation and consultation

Based on the above results, the project team held three evaluation committees of education think tanks in Nanjing, Wuhan, and Beijing, and several rounds of small-scale consultation sessions to discuss and analyze the evaluation results of education think tanks.

(3) Results of evaluation

The project team selected the 2019 CETTE education think tanks

Chapter 3 China Education Think Tank Evaluation and 2019 Rankings

through subjective and objective evaluation methods with a combination of data collection and expert evaluation analysis. The results are as follows:

1. Education think tanks on the core list of CETTE

Table 3 – 2   Education Think Tanks Directly Under the Government on the Core List of CETTE (in alphabetical order by name)

Name of the education think tank
National Center for Education Development Research
National Institute of Education Sciences

Source: prepared by this project team.

Table 3 – 3   Education Think Tanks Directly under the Local Education Institutes on the Core List of CETTE (in alphabetical order by name)

Name of the education think tank
Beijing Academy of Education Sciences
ChongQing Research Academy of Education Sciences
Guangdong Academy of Education
Hunan Academy of Education Sciences
Jiangsu Academy of Education Sciences
Shanghai Academy of Education Sciences
Zhejiang Research Institute of Education Sciences

Source: prepared by this project team.

Table 3 – 4   Internationally Co-Constructed Education Think Tanks on the Core List of CETTE (in alphabetical order by name)

Name of the education think tank
UNESCO International Research and Training Center for Rural Education (UNESCO-INRULED), Beijing Normal University

Table Continued

Name of the education think tank
International Center for Higher Education Innovation under the auspices of UNESCO, Southern University of Science and Technology
Research Institute for International and Comparative Education, Shanghai Normal University (UNESCO International Center of Teacher Education, Shanghai Normal University)

Source: Prepared by Project Team.

Table 3-5　Double First-Class University Education Think Tanks on the Core List of CETTE (in alphabetical order by name)

Name of the education think tank
China Institute for Educational and Finance Research, Peking University
Capital Institute for Economics of Education, Beijing Normal University
Institute of Education and Social Development, Beijing Normal University
Collaborative Innovation Center for Quality Monitoring of China's Basic Education, Beijing Normal University
China Research Institute of Rural Education, Northeast Normal University
National Institute of Educational Policy Research, East China Normal University
The Institute of Curriculum & Instruction, East China Normal University
Education Governance and Think Tanks Research Institute, Central China Normal University
Centre for Research and Evaluation of Higher Education, Nanjing University
Institute of Moral Education, Nanjing Normal University
Institute of Education, Tsinghua University
Capital Educational Policy and Law Research Institute, Capital Normal University
Southwest National Education and Psychological Research Center, Southwest University
Institute of China's Science and Education Strategy, Zhejiang University

Source: Prepared by Project Team.

Table 3-6　Local University Education Think Tanks on the Core List of CETTE (in alphabetical order by name)

Name of the education think tank
Anhui Education Development Research Center, Anhui Normal University
Guangxi Nationalities Education Development Research Center, Guangxi Normal University

Chapter 3 China Education Think Tank Evaluation and 2019 Rankings ▶▶▶

Table Continued

Name of the education think tank
The Research Center of Education Policy, Guangzhou University
Institute of Education Reform and Development, Hainan Normal University
Anhui Big Data Research Center for University Management, Huaibei Normal University
Jiangsu Institute of Education Modernization
Institute of Education Policy, Jiangsu University
Xiangyu Basic Education Practice Research Institute, Tianjin Normal University
Tianjin Education Development Research Center, Tianjin University of Science & Technology
Northwest Minorities Education Development Research Center, Northwest Normal University
Institute of Minorities Education Policy and Law, South-Central University for Nationalities

Source: Prepared by Project Team.

Table 3 - 7   Social / Enterprise Education Think Tanks on the Core List of CETTE (in alphabetical order by name)

Name of the education think tank
21 st Century Education Research Institute
Changjiang Education Research Institute
China Education 30 Forum

Source: Prepared by Project Team.

2. Education think tanks selected for CETTE source

Table 3 - 8   Think Tanks of Local Scientific Research Institutes Selected for CETTE (in alphabetical order by name)

Name of the education think tank
Chengdu Research Academy of Education Science
Fujian Research Academy of Education Science
Guangzhou Institute of Educational Research
Hubei Research Academy of Education Science
Jilin Academy of Education Sciences
Shandong Provincial Institute of Education Science
Shenzhen Education Science Research Institute

Source: Prepared by Project Team.

Table 3 – 9　Double First-Class University Think Tanks Selected for
　　　　　　 CETTE (in alphabetical order by name)

Name of the education think tank
Teacher Education Research Center, Beijing Normal University
International and Comparative Education Research Center, Beijing Normal University
National Vocation Education Research Center, Beijing Normal University
Higher Education Research Institute, Fudan University
Education Reform and Development Research Center, Henan University
Hubei Education Policy Research Center, Central China Normal University
Technology and Basic Education Balanced Development Provincial and Ministerial Co-construction Collaborative Innovation Center, Central China Normal University
Education Leadership and Management Research Institute, Nanjing Normal University
Marine Education Research Center, Ningbo University
Education and Rule of Law Research Center, Shaanxi Normal University
Western China Education Research Center, Shaanxi Normal University
World First-class University Research Center, Shanghai Jiaotong University
Education Policy Research Center, Tongji University
Higher Education Quality and Evaluation Research Institute, Xiamen University
Educational Law Research Institute, Renmin University of China
Education Development and Public Policy Research Center, Renmin University of China

Source: Prepared by Project Team.

Table 3 – 10　Local University Education Think Tanks on the Core List
　　　　　　　of CETTE (in alphabetical order by name)

Name of the education think tank
Institute of Higher Education, Dongguan University of Technology
ASEAN Education Research Institute, Guangxi Normal University
Research Center for Educational Informatization and Balanced Development of Basic Education, Hubei University
Hubei Research Center for Teacher Education, Hubei University of Education
Nanjing Education Think Tank, Nanjing Xiaozhuang University
Research Institute of Vocational Education and Teacher Training, Tianjin University of Technology and Education

Chapter 3   China Education Think Tank Evaluation and 2019 Rankings

Table Continued

Name of the education think tank
Research Center for the Development of Higher Education in Beijing, Tianjin and Hebei, Tangshan Normal University
Institute of Higher Education, Wuhan Institute of Technology

Source: Prepared by Project Team.

Table 3 - 11   Social / Enterprise Education Think Tanks Selected for CETTE (in alphabetical order by name)

Name of the education think tank
Square Creative Education Technology (Beijing) Co., Ltd.
Sunglory Education Institute
China Education Improving Institute

Source: Prepared by Project Team.

(4) Influence evaluation by item

Through the indicator system in the previous annual report, the influence indicator reached 0.4778. After a slight adjustment of the indicator system, the influence indicator weight was calculated to be 0.4832, which proves once again how a think tank ultimately plays a role is reflected in its influence. To this end, in this evaluation process, we combined data analysis and expert scoring to sort out the current Chinese think tanks in terms of decision-making influence, social influence, and outcome influence. The reason for not considering the assessment of international influence is that China's education think tanks have not yet fully performed their functions of "public diplomacy" and there are few examples of education think tanks going abroad. In addition, the impact of results has been increased, and data has been extracted from the "academic achievements" in the first-level indicator "achievement indicators". The reason for this consideration is that in the long run when research results are released and disseminated they are likely to draw attention from academic circles to certain educational issues, which will eventually become the driving force for decision-making. The results are as follows.

1. Decision-making influence

Table 3 – 12

Rank	Name of the education think tank
1	National Institute of Education Sciences
2	National Center for Education Development Research
3	Institute of Education and Social Development, Beijing Normal University
4	China Institute for Educational and Finance Research, Peking University
5	National Institutes of Educational Policy Research, East China Normal University
6	Changjiang Education Research Institute
7	Institute of Education, Tsinghua University
8	UNESCO International Research and Training Center for Rural Education (UNESCO-INRULED), Beijing Normal University
9	Institute of Rural Education Development, Northeast Normal University
10	Research Institute for International and Comparative Education, Shanghai Normal University (UNESCO International Center of Teacher Education, Shanghai Normal University)

2. Social influence

Table 3 – 13

Rank	Name of the education think tank
1	Changjiang Education Research Institute
2	21st Century Education Research Institute
3	China Education 30 Forum

Table Continued

Rank	Name of the education think tank
4	National Institute of Education Sciences
5	China Institute of Rural Education Development, Northeast Normal University
6	National Institute of Educational Policy Research, East China Normal University
7	Collaborative Innovation Center for Quality Monitoring of China's Basic Education, Beijing Normal University
8	Education Governance and Think Tanks Research Institute, Central China Normal University
9	Beijing Academy of Education Sciences
10	China Education Improving Institute

3. Achievement influence

Table 3 – 14

Rank	Name of the education think tank
1	National Institute of Education Sciences
2	Institute of Education, Tsinghua University
3	Institute of Education and Social Development, Beijing Normal University
4	China Institute of Rural Education Development, Northeast Normal University
5	Changjiang Education Research Institute
6	National Institute of Educational Policy Research, East China Normal University
7	Capital Institute for Economics of Education, Beijing Normal University
8	Southwest National Education and Psychological Research Center, Southwest University
9	Institute of Moral Education, Nanjing Normal University
10	China Institute for Educational and Finance Research, Peking University

(5) Data analysis of think tanks selected for CETTE

1. Regional distribution

A total of 74 education think tanks have been selected by the China Education Think Tank Evaluation Platform (CETTE), covering 20 provinces and cities including Beijing, Shanghai, Hubei, Jiangsu,

Zhejiang, Guangdong, Shaanxi, and Chongqing. In terms of quantity, Beijing, Hubei, Shanghai, and Jiangsu rank in the top four, which is also inseparable from the science and education background of these four provinces. Beijing is far ahead with 20 education think tanks selected, which also reflects the status of Beijing's education center and has a close relationship with the gradual classification of education think tanks in universities such as Beijing Normal University. Hubei is followed by 9 education think tanks, mainly because of the guiding role of Central China Normal University's Education Governance and Think Tank Research Institute in central China, which has made great progress in the construction of education think tanks in this region. Shanghai and Jiangsu are two provinces (cities) with strong education. East China Normal University, Shanghai Normal University and other universities have rich experience in the construction of education think tanks. Jiangsu Province, under the guidance of the Propaganda Department of the Provincial Party Committee, has built think tanks in all aspects and has made great progress.

However, statistics show that there are still more than ten provinces, municipalities and autonomous regions that have not yet established systematic, reasonable, and effective education think tanks. In the course of this survey, the project team repeatedly searched some provinces, but still could not find a representative education think tank. Therefore, except for Hong Kong, Macao and Taiwan regions, there were 11 provinces and cities without education think tanks being selected. Among them, some think tanks were selected last year but they failed to carry out effective work throughout this year, and they were eliminated as "empty think tanks". Also some provinces and cities have no active

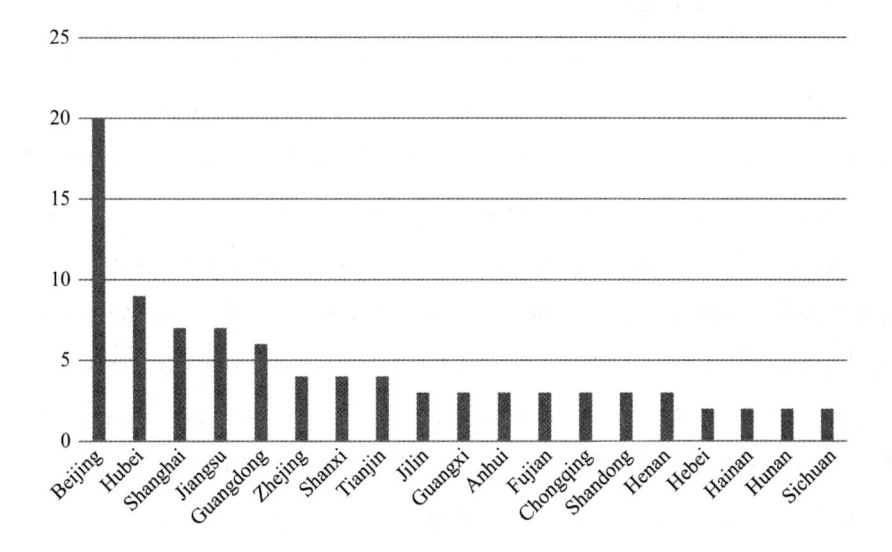

Figure 3 – 2　Regional distribution of Chinese education think tanks

think tanks. These provinces are mainly concentrated in the central and western regions of China. It is related to the lack of local science and education resources and may also be related to the degree of understanding of think tanks by local governments and functional departments. The lack of education think tanks in the central and western regions has resulted in the inability of educational policy researchers to effectively participate in the process of modernization of educational governance capacity and governance system, which will further hinder the development of education in the central and western regions. This will also become the future national policy orientation and need to be further improved. For a long time to come, it will be a long-term growth point to guide the educational institutions in the central and western regions to turn to education think tanks, and at the same time to support the regional universities' education think tanks to actively participate in regional governance.

2. education think tank categories

In terms of categories, university think tanks are still the main component. In this statistics, university think tanks include internationally-constructed education think tanks, double first-class university think tanks and other think tanks for university education, with a total of 52, accounting for 70% of the total number of think tanks selected. Among them double first-class university think tanks have more channels to report, so they have undoubtedly become the most important part of the selected education think tanks. The local university think tanks are experiencing the hard transformation process. Traditionally, the academies of education tend to focus on micro-specific issues such as curriculum and teaching, and rarely care about major educational strategic issues such as regional education reform. The survey shows that at present, Beijing, Shanghai, Guangdong, Jiangsu, Chongqing, and other provinces and cities with more developed educational resources have formed a two-wheel drive of combing macroeconomic decision-making with educational research on specific issues, but many academies are still working on traditional fields. Social education think tanks are still growing slowly, which is in sharp contrast with the development of social think tanks in the political and economic fields. Internationally-constructed education think tanks, as an important classification item in this research report, needs to be more active to fully utilize their unique international resources.

In this category, local university education think tanks accounted for 26%. The project team believes that this type of education think tank will become an important driving force for local education governance. This type of local university education think tank is different from the double

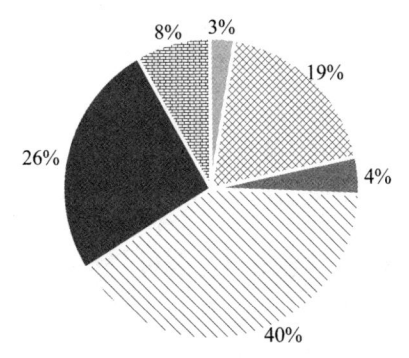

Chapter 3 China Education Think Tank Evaluation and 2019 Rankings

- Education Think Tanks Directly Under the Government
- Education Think Tanks Directly under the Local Education Institutes
- Internationally Co-Constructed Education Think Tanks
- Double First-Class University Education Think Tanks
- Local University Education Think Tanks
- Social / Enterprise Education Think Tanks

Figure 3 – 3 Analysis of education think tank categories

first-class university education think tank. Their focus is more on local education policy-making and education reform. At present, all parts of the country are steadily advancing the implementation of the spirit of the National Education Conference. To implement, research, and do a good job in cities and regions, the only thing that can be relied upon is education think tanks within the regions and cities. Therefore, in the future, this type of think tank will also become a breakthrough point for the rapid growth of education think tanks.

Chapter 4　Main Research Topics of Education Think Tanks in 2019

The year 2019 is of great significance for China's education. This year's provinces, municipalities and autonomous regions have successively held provincial and municipal education conferences to implement the central education policies. Education think tanks have actively participated in governance in this process, advising on political advice, theoretical innovation, guidance of public opinion, social services, public relations and diplomacy played an important role. During the year, education think tanks mainly focused on the following issues.

Figure 4-1　Keywords of education think tank research in 2019

Chapter 4　Main Research Topics of Education Think Tanks in 2019

(1) Education modernization and educational governance

At the beginning of 2019, the Central Committee of the Communist Party of China and the State Council issued and issued *China Education Modernization* 2035 and *Implementation Plan for Accelerating the Modernization of Education* (2018 – 2022), which aroused strong attention from all walks of life. Subsequently, various education think tanks carried out a series of studies, and formed a series of results in the fields of document interpretation and implementation. In this process, a series of high-end education think tanks, such as the National Education Development Research Center, the Chinese Academy of Education Sciences, the Beijing Normal University China Education and Social Development Institute, and the Changjiang Education Research Institute, have successively published a series of articles[1] on important newspapers such as *Guangming Daily* and *China Education Daily* and played a good role in guiding public opinions.

The Office of the Chinese Academy of Education Sciences and the Office of the National Education Science Planning Leadership Group held the "China Education Science Forum" in Beijing on April 17, 2019,

---

[1]　Only articles by researchers from selected education think tanks are included here. Some of them are: Gu Mingyuan, "How to advance education modernization in new age", *Guangming Daily*, March 5, 2019; Tan Songhua, "Fully understanding the four key points of education modernization", *Guangming Daily*, March 5, 2019; Zhou Hongyu & Liu Dawei, "New goals and new journey of education modernization in new age", *Chinese Education Daily*, April 1, 2019; Xue Eryong, "Starting the new journey of advancing education modernization in new age", *People's Political Consultative Daily*, Feb 27, 2019; Hujuan, "Overcoming three difficulties of higher education modernization", *Guangming Daily*, April 23, 2019; Li Liguo, "Values of university governance modernization", *Guangming Daily*, Nov. 19, 2019.

focusing on the path to implement China's education modernization 2035. In terms of theoretical research, the policy interpretation and related research on education modernization 2035 has continued from the beginning of the year to the end of 2019, reflecting the continuous attention of education think tanks on this hot issue. The main focus was on the modernization of education at different stages, such as preschool education modernization and compulsory education modernization and vocational education modernization. On December 8, 2019, the China

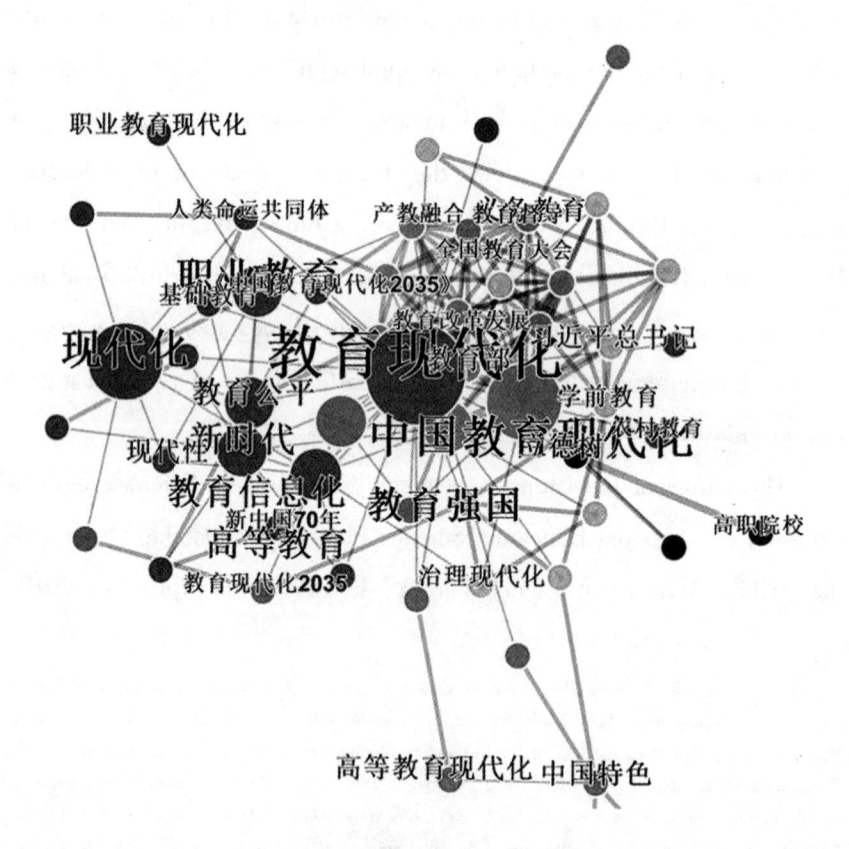

Figure 4-2　Keyword co-occurrence of research on "education modernization" in 2019

Chapter 4　Main Research Topics of Education Think Tanks in 2019　▶▶▶

Education 30 Forum hosted the annual conference with the theme of "Science and Technology Development and Educational Reform", focusing on the changes in science and technology and the ecology of education and the challenges brought by science and technology development to education. This forum was a remarkable event on education modernization at the end of this year.

The modernization of education is inseparable from the modernization of the governance system. Since the release of *China Education Modernization 2035* at the beginning of the year, some education think tanks have conducted studies on modernization of education governance system and published their research findings. With the convening of the Fourth Plenary Session of the Nineteenth Central Committee of the Party at the end of October 2019, more education think tanks successively carried out research on the modernization of the national education governance system and the modernization of governance capabilities. [①] On November 9, 2019, the Changjiang Education Research Institute took the theme of "Deepening Educational Reform, Accelerating the Modernization of Educational Governance System and Governance Ability", and held the "2019 Education Think Tank and Educational Governance Roundtable Forum in Beijing" in Beijing. Xu Hui, Zhang

---

[①] education think tanks have conducted studies on this topic, such as Zhou Hongyu, "Deepen the reform of 'decentralization of service' in education and accelerate the modernization of education governance", *Education Research*, (3), 2019; Zhou Hongyu, "Strengthening educational scientific research, helping modernize education governance system", *Education Research*, (11), 2019; Cui Baoshi, "The blueprint of the basic system and governance system of China's educational scientific research in the new era", *Education Research*, (11), 2019; Mo Lan, "Educational governance isn't just seeking solutions within school fences", *Guangming Daily*, Nov. 19, 2019; University governance: from experience to science", *Guangming Daily*, Dec. 2, 2019 among others.

Li, Zhang Minxuan, Zhou Hongyu, Peng Binbai and other experts and scholars talked about the educational reform measures on the implementation of the spirit of the Fourth Plenary Session of the 19th Central Committee of the CPC Central Committee. This hotspot issue will become the focus of attention of education think tanks at present and for a long time to come.

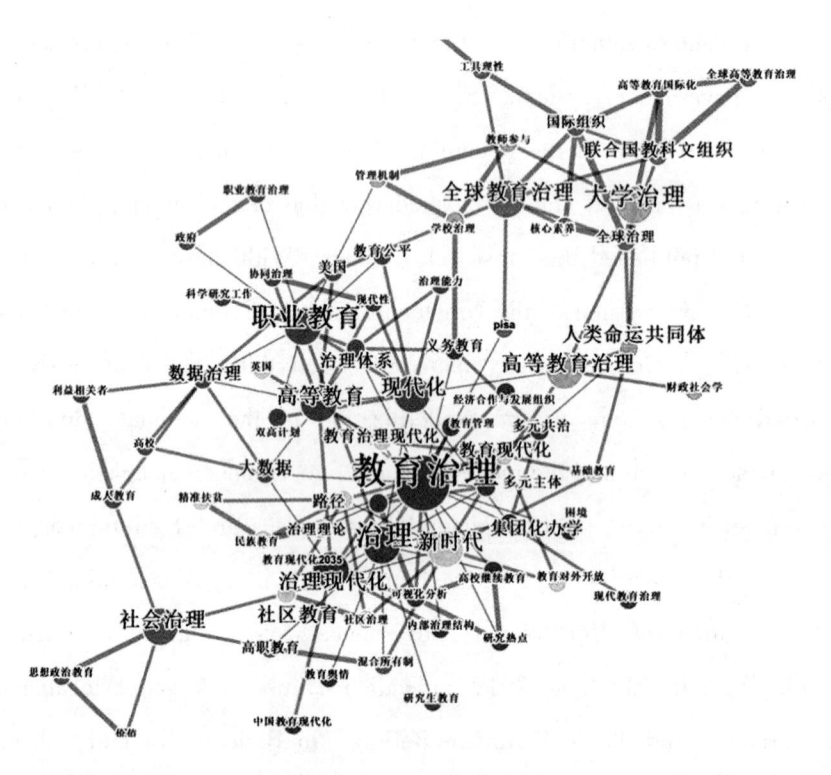

Figure 4-3 Keyword co-occurrence of research on "education governance" in 2019

(2) Education legal system construction

At the beginning of 2019, a national conference on the education law and policy was convened. The meeting emphasized the need to

Chapter 4　Main Research Topics of Education Think Tanks in 2019　▶▶▶

comprehensively promote the administration of education according to law, accelerate the pace of legislative work, and provide policy and relevant laws to guarantees education reform and development. During the year, issues related to education laws that have drawn most attention include the issue of preschool education legislation and the right to education punishment. On January 5, 2019, the China Academy of Education and Social Development of Beijing Normal University and the Capital Institute of Education and Economics co-hosted a seminar on "Deepening Reform and Development of Preschool Education" and discussed on issues related to the management system, investment system and park management system of preschool education. During the following two sessions, the leaders of education think tanks such as Pang Lijuan and Zhou Hongyu, who are representatives of the National People's Congress, proposed to accelerate the legislation of preschool education law and amend the Teachers Law to give teachers the right to education punishment during the meeting, which aroused widespread attention in the society. Focusing on the issue of the rule of law in education and the specific points involved, the above-mentioned education think tanks have carried out in-depth research directly guided by the Teacher Work Department of the Ministry of Education, and finally formed special reports, papers, and other forms of results for submission to relevant functional departments. In July 2019, the Central Committee of the Communist Party of China and the State Council issued the document *Opinions on Deepening the Reform of Education and Teaching and Improving the Quality of Compulsory Education in an All-round Way*, which explicitly proposed to guarantee teachers' right to education punishment in accordance with the law. This also reflects the important role of education think tanks in influencing education policy.

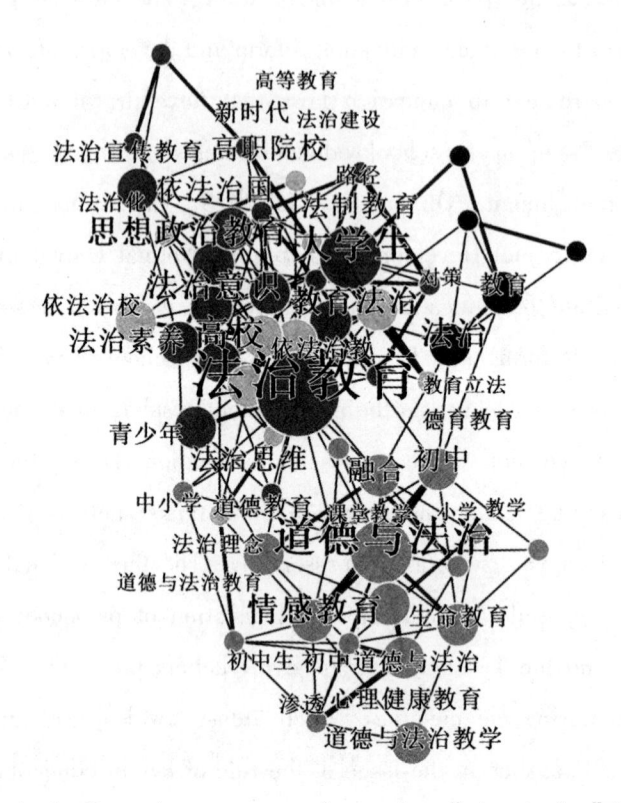

Figure 4-4 Keyword co-occurrence of research on "education law" in 2019

(3) Cultivating ideals of talents

At the National Education Conference, President Xi Jinping emphasized that "it is necessary to focus on the fundamental question of cultivating what kind of talents, how to cultivate talents, and cultivating talents for whom, to uphold the principle of cultivating ideals of talents, strengthen ideological and political work in schools, promote educational

Chapter 4　Main Research Topics of Education Think Tanks in 2019　▶▶▶

reform, and accelerate the modernization of education."① Therefore, in 2019, relevant education think tanks such as the China Institute of Education and Social Development of Beijing Normal University and the Institute of Moral Education of Nanjing Normal University and other institutions attached great importance to the issue of cultivating ideals of talents, conducted various academic seminars, and published research

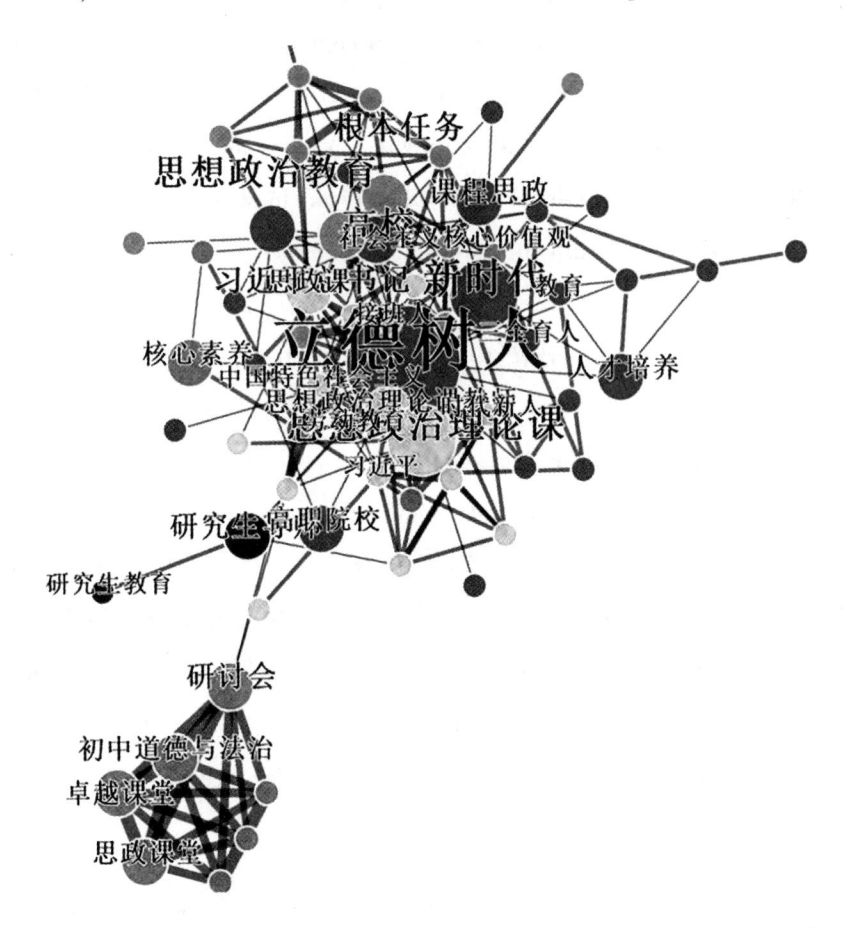

Figure 4 – 5　Keyword co-occurrence of research on "cultivating ideals of talents" in 2019

---

① *People's Daily*, Sept. 11, 2018.

results,① giving full play to the role and value of education think tanks in the three dimensions including theoretical innovation, public opinion guidance and social service. The think tanks' appeal is also combined with the government's demands, and in 2019, they successively issued the *Opinions on Strengthening the Construction of Teachers in the Ideological and Political Theory Course in the New Age of Primary and Secondary Schools* and *The Views on Strengthening and Improving the Construction of Teachers' Morality and Style in the New Age*. The introduction of related documents provided a basis for policies related to cultivating ideals of talents and offered an implementation path for realizing the goals of cultivating ideals of talents.

(4) Reducing burden of teachers

The year 2019 is the "grass-roots burden reduction year" proposed by the Central Committee of the Communist Party of China. Therefore, at the National Education Work Conference in early 2019, Minister of Education Chen Baosheng stressed that efforts will be made to reduce the burden on teachers. This topic also became one of the main issues that education think tanks paid attention to. In order to achieve this goal, the Ministry of Education held several seminars, inviting relevant think tank

---

① education think tanks have conducted many studies on this topic. Among them are Xue Eryong, "Promoting all-round development through education", *Chinese Education Daily*, Oct, 8, 2019; Feng Jianjun, "The new-age meaning and implementation route of cultivating ideals of talents", *People's Education*, (18), 2019; Feng Jianjun, "Establishing the mechanism of systematic implementation of cultivating ideals of talents", *Journal of National College of Education Administration*, (4), 2019; Zhou Hongyu, "Strengthening research and interpretation of President Xi's important discussions on education", *Chinese Higher Education*, (19), 2019.

Chapter 4　Main Research Topics of Education Think Tanks in 2019　▶▶▶

members to participate in the meeting and express their opinions. Relevant education think tanks also summed up the experience of different regions on reducing burden of teachers, learned from the measures taken by western developed countries in this regard, visited a large number of primary and secondary schools, published articles in newspapers and periodicals to guide public opinions[①], and wrote relevant research reports to the relevant departments of the Ministry of Education. Finally, with the joint efforts of many parties, at the end of 2019, the General Office of the Central Committee of the Communist Party of China and the General Office of the State Council issued *Several Opinions on Reducing the Burden of Teachers in Primary and Secondary Schools and Further Creating a*

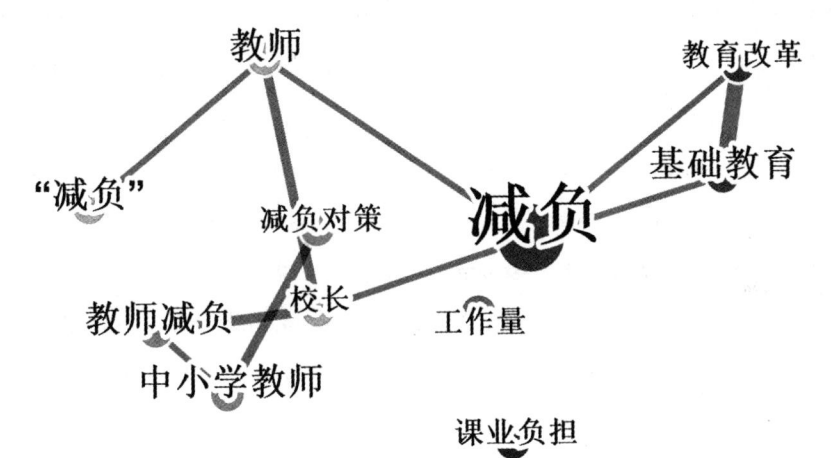

Figure 4-6　Keyword co-occurrence of research on "reducing burden of teachers" in 2019

[①] education think tanks have conducted many studies on this topic. Among them are Ye Meijin & Wu Daguang, "Reducing burden on teachers, expanding the space for development", *Guangming Daily*, March 12, 2019; Wu Zebin, "Reducing burden on teachers: The goal is increasing potential, the key is institution", *Guang Ming Daily*, April 2, 2019; "Three 'returning' must be done to reduce burden on teachers", *Guang Ming Daily*, April 2, 2019; Zhou Hongyu, "Fundamentals should be done to reduce burden on teachers", *Guangming Daily*, Oct. 31, 2019.

· 111 ·

Good Environment for Education and Teaching to reduce the burden on primary and secondary schools, to "bring schools back to order and give time back to teachers".

(5) Education internationalization

Education internationalization is an inevitable choice for a powerful country in education. Among the ten strategic tasks of *China Education Modernization* 2035, Article 9 clearly states that a new pattern of education opening up must be created. In the document *Implementation Plan for Accelerating the Modernization of Education* (2018 – 2022), Article 9 of the ten key tasks is also to "promote joint construction of the 'Belt and Road' educational action". In 2019, some education think tanks have paid attention to this hot issue. For example, Shanghai Normal University Institute of International and Comparative Education (UN Teacher Education Center) devoted to the international surveys such as the International Student Assessment Project (PISA) and Teaching and Learning International Survey (TALIS), promoted the "Sino-British Mathematics Teacher Exchange Program". When the PISA results were announced at the end of 2019, the issue aroused heated debate in the academic community. On this basis, this center also published a series of research reports and articles on various international exchanges on education. Some decision-making consultative reports have been affirmed by the state, provincial and ministerial agencies. In addition, Changjiang Education Research Institute worked further on this issue and held the "Belt and Road Education Think Tank Dialogue", which were also recognized by relevant departments of the Ministry of Education.

Chapter 4　Main Research Topics of Education Think Tanks in 2019　▶▶▶

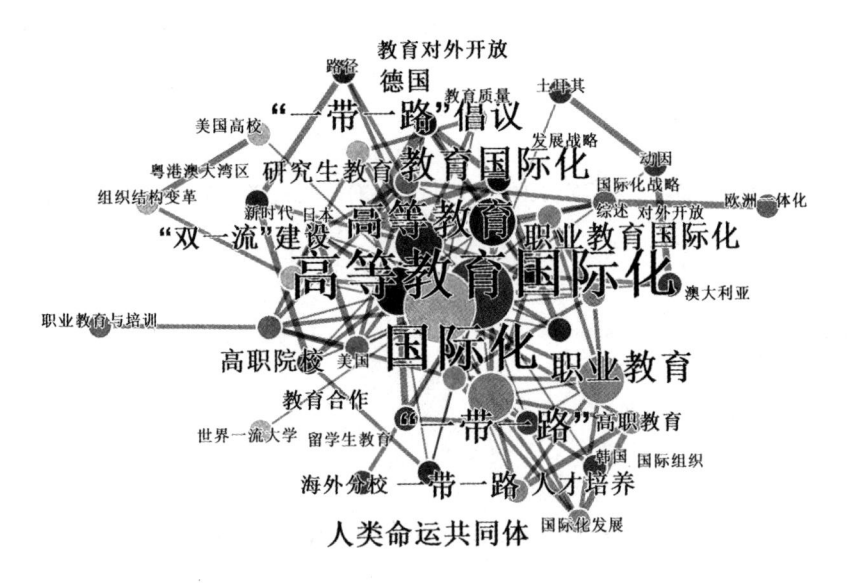

Figure 4 – 7　Keyword co-occurrence of research on "education internationalization" in 2019

Of course, the above mentioned only included education policy research conducted the selected education think tanks. In addition, issues such as integration of production and education, college entrance examination reform, school safety, education for poverty alleviation, and family education are also the focus of the think tanks. For local education think tanks, they will pay more attention to the implementation of central policies in the region, as well as the hot and difficult issues of education in the region.

Chapter 5 Characteristics of Chinese Education Think Tanks in 2019

(1) More effective advice and consultation

The year 2019 has special significance for Chinese education. In order to implement the spirit of the National Education Conference, various provinces and cities have successively held education conferences to implement education in the region. At the same time, the release of *China Education Modernization 2035* has also promoted more education think tanks to invest in education policy research with greater enthusiasm. In 2019, in view of the hotspot issues and difficult issues of national education in the region, more education think tanks have clearly identified their positions, made recommendations for consultations, and gained more recognition and adoption by government functional departments.

Beginning in early 2019, various education think tanks have successively organized staff to publish reading articles on *China Education Modernization 2035* on *People's Daily*, *Guangming Daily*, *China Education Daily* and various professional academic journals, which

Chapter 5　Characteristics of Chinese Education Think Tanks in 2019

aroused attention to the issue of China's education modernization and build a good public opinion foundation for the advancement of *China's Education Modernization 2035*.

During the two sessions, education think tanks such as the Changjiang Education Research Institute, Central China Normal University's Education Governance and Think Tank Institute and others worked on proposals of educational governance reform of decentralization of management service, and expand the autonomy of self-sponsored colleges and universities. The proposals on reform of "decentralization of management services" and promotion of modernization of education governance were received and accepted by the Ministry of Education. For this reason, the Ministry of Education replied on August 22, 2019 that it will deepen the reform of decentralization of management service through the measures of "promoting the government to transform education administrative functions, implement and expand school autonomy" "creating a good institutional environment for social organizations to participate in education governance", and "de-administration of higher education, educator-based school" "accelerating the improvement of the national education standard system" "exploring the 'Internet + Education Supervision New System'" "optimizing the education service environment" "accelerating the educational legislative process" "overcoming the 'five stubbornness' problem" and "building an integrated education supervision system". [1] This policy proposal also promoted the Ministry of Education

---

[1]　Reply to Recommendation No. 4835 of the Second Session of the Thirteenth National People's Congress. http://www.moe.gov.cn/jyb_xxgk/xxgk_jyta/jyta_zfs/201910/t20191025_405223.html.

to formulate the "2019 Annual Task List for Deepening the Reform of Decentralization of Management and Service in education field", clarifying 30 key reform tasks, policy measures and division of responsibilities in 5 areas, which provided a decision basis for precise education governance. In terms of macro policy research, education think tanks including Institute of Education and Social Development, Beijing Normal University, National Institute of Educational Policy Research, East China Normal University, Western China Education Research Center, Shaanxi Normal University, Tianjin Education Development Research Center, Tianjin University of Science and Technology, Xiangyu Basic Education Practice Research Institute, Tianjin Normal University, Marine Education Research Center, Ningbo University, The Research Center of Education Policy, Guangzhou University, Beijing Academy of Educational Sciences, Jiangsu Institute of Education Modernization started from the national strategy of "four points, one line, one side" and conducted in-depth investigations and addressed the issues of integrated education in Beijing, Tianjin and Hebei, education in the Guangdong-Hong Kong-Macao Greater Bay Area, integrated education in the Yangtze River Delta, education cooperation among areas along the Yangtze River Economic Belt, education cooperation among countries along the Belt and Road. Some relevant results were approved and adopted by leaders of the state and local governments. Among the several important education think tanks mentioned above, Institute of Education and Social Development of Beijing Normal University prepared 17 advisory reports which were approved for adoption by local government leaders at different levels and 6 were approved for adoption by the Party and national leaders. National Institute of Educational Policy Research of East China Normal University prepared 42 advisory reports that were approved for adoption by central and municipal government leaders, among which 2 reports were approved for adoption by central government leaders. Research Institute of Rural Education, Northeast Normal University due to their discipline advantage, prepared 13 advisory reports, among which one report was approved with positive response by national leaders. Changjiang Education Research Institute submitted 46 advisory and consultation reports, among which 25 received positive comments, 10 reports were approved by the Party and national leaders. More local education think tanks and local educational institutions drafted the implementation outline and road map of education 2035 on the basis of implementing the spirit of local education conferences, provided research reports for local education decision-making consultation, and played an important role in serving local society. *Education Decision-making Reference* prepared by Hunan Academy of Education Sciences received one approval from national leaders and many pieces of advice were adopted by education policy documents of Hunan provincial government. Authorized by Education Department of Jiangsu Provincial Government, Jiangsu Academy of Education Sciences undertook the work of compiling *Jiangsu Education Modernization 2035* and submitted many advisory reports to Jiangsu provincial government and the provincial education department and received one approval from the major provincial leaders. Tianjin Education Development Research Center of Tianjin University of Science and Technology joined the work of compiling a series of documents including Tainjin Education Modernization 2013, the plan of five-year implementation, the three-year action plan of basic education balanced development, and played a role of think tank for Tianjin education advice and consultation. Anhui Big Data Research Center for University Management, Huaibei Normal University finished 2018 *Higher Education Satisfaction Survey and Analysis Report of Anhui Province*, which became the important reference for Education Department of Anhui Province to study and judge higher education quality. It also compiled *Huaibei Rural Areas Renovation Strategic Plan* (2018 – 2022), which became the important reference document for rural renovation of Huaibei City. Nanjing Academy of Education Sciences compiled Nanjing Education Modernization 2035, providing reference and pointing direction for the future development of Nanjing education. Nanjing Education Think Tank of Nanjing Xiaozhuang University wrote Research Report on Development of Schools Run by Local People, which was approved by Nanjing Municipal Bureau of Finance and provided theoretical foundation and decision-making reference for the adjustment of funding for Nanjing schools run by local people in 2019. In general, the main focus of education think tanks in 2019 mainly was on the implementation of the spirit of the National Education Conference, drafting and planning of education modernization in 2035, the steady development of balanced compulsory education, and the further advancement of the construction of law in education. With the continuous awareness of the concept of think tanks, and the understanding and acceptance of think tank functions by education think tanks, the decision-making consultations of each think tank have gradually been refined and targeted, that is, high-end education think tanks are aligned with national macro education policy issues, and regional education think tanks are more concerned about policy implementation and educational practice, which also further improves the efficiency of advice and consultation.

(2) More diverse collaborations

Since 2019, the cooperation of education think tanks has become more diverse. This includes cooperation between think tanks and think tanks, cooperation between think tanks and the media, and cooperation between think tanks and the government.

The cooperation between media especially new media and think tanks has further promoted the social influence of think tanks. The cooperation between think tanks and the media can make the dissemination and diffusion of think tank research no longer a one-way behavior, but a kind of "coupling" process—the research findings of think tank were disseminated on various platforms and meanwhile aroused interactions so that the research findings spread nationwide. [1] Guided by this cutting-edge thinking, many education think tanks have set up cooperation channels with the media, and used the media's dissemination power to expand the influence of think tanks. In this regard, *Guangming Daily* was an example. In October 2019, *Guangming Daily* Basic Education Think Tank Committee was established. Its goal was to focus on China's basic education policy decision-making research and education reform practices, focus on and track education hotspot issues and difficult issues, and respond to public expectations for quality education in a timely manner; *Guangzhou Daily* Data and Digit Institute (GDI Think

---

[1] Zhu Ruijuan, "Communication mechanism of the cooperation between new media and western well-known think tanks—examples of communication related to 'Belt and Road' construction research findings", *Modern Communication*, (4), 2018.

Tank) also cooperated with more than 20 education think tanks, such as the Changjiang Education Research Institute, to develop and release products such as the "Applied University Rankings" "Higher Vocational College Rankings" and "Private Higher Education Development Report", and further expanded the social influence of the results by virtue of their media advantage. The influence of new media cannot be underestimated. Square Creative Education Technology (Beijing) Co., Ltd. and Changjiang Education Research Institute signed a cooperation agreement in January 2019 to work together to collect education data collection, develop research reports, submit internal references and use the "First Reading EDU" official account of Square Creative Education Technology (Beijing) Co., Ltd. to promote the research results of think tanks. Among them, the "Selected List of 40 Educators in the 40 Years of Reform and Opening", jointly selected by education think tanks such as Changjiang Education Research Institute and Square Creative Education Technology (Beijing) Co., Ltd. was read for more than 88,000 times on official accounts and was republished by multiple official accounts.

Cooperation among education think tanks also became more active in 2019. In September 2019, Twenty-one education think tanks including Changjiang Education Research Institute, School of Education of Tianjin University, School of Education of Shaanxi Normal University, Graduate School of Education of Beijing Foreign Studies University, School of Education of Central China Normal University, School of Education of Guangzhou University, School of Education of Henan University, School of Education Sciences of Hainan Normal University initiated the establishment of the "Belt and Road" Education Think Tank Alliance to

Chapter 5 Characteristics of Chinese Education Think Tanks in 2019 ▶▶▶

promote education cooperation among countries along the "Belt and Road". This is currently the largest alliance of education think tanks in China, including many domestic universities, educational research institutions, media, and others, and has formed a greater influence. Among them, the Changjiang Education Research Institute played an important role in organization, planning and coordination. In January 2019, three education think tanks including Jiangsu University, Jiangsu Institute of Modern Education, and Yangtze River Education Research Institute jointly organized the "Zhenjiang · Changjiang Education Forum". Zhou Hongyu, member of the Standing Committee of the National People's Congress and vice chairman of the Chinese Education Society, Hu Jinbo, Secretary of the Party Committee of Nanjing University, vice chairman of the CPPCC of Jiangsu Province, President Meng Fanhua of Capital Normal University, President Yan Xiaohong of Jiangsu University, Professor Sui Yifan of Zhejiang University, Professor Yan Guangcai of East China Normal University and other experts and scholars discussed the construction of high-level universities. In March, People's Education Publishing House and Changjiang Education Research Institute jointly held the "Beijing Changjiang Education Forum". Experts at the meeting made a pre-judgment on the new situation of education reform and development. The organizer also released the *China Education Policy Proposal* (2019 Edition), *China Education Index* (2019 Edition), *Top Ten Educational Keywords in* 2019. Zhu Yongxin, Member of the Standing Committee of the CPPCC, Deputy Secretary-General, Vice Chairman of the Democratic Progressive Central Committee, Zhou Hongyu, Standing Committee member of the National People's Congress, Deputy Director of Standing Committee of Hubei

Provincial People's Congress and other experts or scholars attended the meeting and made keynote speeches. In April, Nanjing Xiaozhuang University, Huazhong Normal University Education Governance and Think Tank Research Institute, Changjiang Education Research Institute, and Zhongguancun Internet Innovation Education Center held the "China Education Think Tank Construction Forum". Tan Fangzheng, Deputy Director of the Department of Social Sciences of the Ministry of Education, attended the meeting. The leaders of well-known Chinese think tanks such as National Institute of Education Sciences, Research Institute for International and Comparative Education of Shanghai Normal University, Institute of Education and Social Development of Beijing Normal University, Institute of Moral Education of Nanjing Normal University, Center for Research and Evaluation of Higher Education of Nanjing University and Changjiang Education Research Institute introduced their experience of constructing education think tanks at the meeting. In June, the "Ningbo Yangtze River Education Forum" held by Ningbo University and Changjiang Education Research Institute discussed the role of education in the integration of the Yangtze River Delta. In August, Tianjin University, Tianjin Normal University, and Changjiang Education Research Institute jointly held the "Tianjin Yangtze River Education Forum", focusing on the development strategy of Xiong'an New Area, pooling their wisdom to accelerate the construction of the Xiong'an New Area's educational reform and opening up demonstration area. In September, Shaanxi Normal University and Changjiang Education Research Institute co-organized the "Xi'an Yangtze River Education Forum" to pay close attention to the opportunities of countries along the Belt and Road in the process of education globalization. In October, the

Chapter 5 Characteristics of Chinese Education Think Tanks in 2019 ▶▶▶

"Hainan · Changjiang Education Forum" hosted by Hainan Normal University and Changjiang Education Research Institute was based on the realistic needs of the Hainan Free Trade Pilot Zone. Kang Yaohong, deputy director of the Standing Committee of the Hainan Provincial People's Congress, and other leading experts attended and fully discussed the development strategies of promoting reform and innovation of Hainan education and enhancing the internationalization of Hainan's education. In the same month, the "Tianjin Yangtze River Education Forum" hosted by Tianjin Normal University and Changjiang Education Research Institute took the theme of "Xiongan New District Development Strategy and High Quality Development of Basic Education" and had in-depth discussions on the development of basic education. It can be said that the cooperation between think tanks and think tanks is a win-win mechanism. For high-end education think tanks, it is to further expand the human resources team and tap the research potential of local education think tanks; for local education think tanks, the reporting channels are obtained through co-construction because a vast majority of local education think tanks simply cannot build effective channels on their own. For example, in the process of co-construction with Changjiang Education Research Institute, the Nanjing education think tank of Nanjing Xiaozhuang University won one national leader approval and one provincial and ministerial approval in 2019. From the perspective of the think tank construction capacity of municipal universities, this is a benchmark think tank achievement, because even high-end education think tanks, such as Institute of Education and Social Development, Beijing Normal University and National Institute of Educational Policy Research of East China Normal University only received six and two approvals respectively from national leaders in 2019. It can be seen that the effect of co-construction is immediate. In the future, this model may become an important development direction for the cooperation and construction of education think tanks.

Table 5 – 1　　　　List of sponsors and members of the
"Belt and Road" Education Think Tank Alliance

Number	Name
1	Changjiang Education Research Institute
2	Square Creative Education Technology (Beijing) Co., Ltd.
3	School of Education, Huazhong Normal University
4	Education Governance and Think Tanks Research Institute, Central China Normal University
5	School of Education, Shaanxi Normal University
6	Gradate School of Education, Beijing Foreign Studies University
7	School of Education, Tianjin University
8	School of Education, Tianjin Normal University
9	Tianjin Education Development Research Center, Tianjin University of Science and Technology
10	School of Education, Inner Mongolia Normal University
11	School of Teacher Education, Jiangsu University
12	Education Research Institute, Nanjing Xiaozhuang University
13	Jiangsu Institute of Education Modernization
14	School of Teacher Education, Ningbo University
15	China Innovation and Entrepreneurship Education Research Institute, Wenzhou Medical University
16	School of Education, Guangzhou University
17	Shenzhen Institute, Henan University
18	Academy of Education Sciences, Hainan Normal University
19	School of Education Sciences and Management, Yunnan Normal University
20	Guangxi College of Education
21	*Guangzhou Daily* Data and Digit Institute

Chapter 5 Characteristics of Chinese Education Think Tanks in 2019 ▶▶▶

Cooperation between think tanks and the government is also strengthening. At the end of 2018, under the guidance of National Center for Schooling Development Programme, China Education Think Tank Network and Hainan Oriental City Government jointly organized the "3rd China Education Think Tank Annual Conference and High-end Education Think Tank Helping Free Trade Zone Innovation and Development Seminar", focusing on innovation and development of education in Hainan Pilot Free Trade Zone. In August, the China Education 30 Forum and Tianshui Municipal People's Government co-sponsored the first China West Education Development Forum. The theme of the forum was "Blocking Intergenerational Transmission of Poverty with Education" and the focus were on reform and development of education in the western region as well as suggestions for eradicating poverty and building a well-off society in the western region. The Forum also released *Research Report on Preschool Education in Western China* and *Research Report on Basic Education in Western China*. At the same time, various education think tanks have gradually increased the number of projects commissioned by the government. For example, think tanks such as Changjiang Education Research Institute and the Teacher Education Research Center of Beijing Normal University have been commissioned by the Ministry of Education's Teacher Work Department to carry out the work of revising the Teachers Law. Research Institute of Rural Education of Northeast Normal University accepted 6 projects commissioned by various departments of Ministry of Education including the Teacher Work Department, Policies and Regulations Department, Basic Education Department, and Ethnic Education Department and conducted surveys on rural education policy, teacher quality and the current development of nationalities rural education among others. Jiangsu Institute of Education Modernization was commissioned by the Jiangsu Provincial Department of Education to conduct a feasibility study and risk assessment of the comprehensive reform plan for Jiangsu college entrance examination, which become an important part and support for the Jiangsu Province's college entrance examination reform plan submitted to for the "Deepening Reform Office" of Central Government for approval.

(3) More professional research reports

In the past year, various education think tanks have released a number of educational research reports. At the end of 2018, Collaborative Innovation Center for Quality Monitoring of China's Basic Education of Beijing Normal University, Institute of Education and Social Development of Beijing Normal University, Children and Family Education Research Center of Beijing Normal University and *Family Education Weekly of China Education Newspaper* jointly issued *National Family Education Survey Report* (2018). The report, through a nationwide survey, objectively presented the current status and prominent issues of family education in China, and provided a scientific basis for scientific research and related policies and regulations of family education. China Institute of Rural Education Development, of Northeast Normal University released *China Rural Education Development Report 2019* in January 2019. The report used national statistics and domestic survey data to present the current situation and achievements of rural education development, problems and challenges, and responses and prospects, which constituted an overview of China's rural education in

Chapter 5 Characteristics of Chinese Education Think Tanks in 2019 ▶▶▶

2018. China Institute of Moral Education of Nanjing Normal University actively participated in the construction of children moral development database. Following the release of *Chinese Children Moral Development Report 2017*, it further undertook the drafting and planning of documents on moral development of children commissioned by the Central Civilization Office, playing an important consultative role of ideological and moral construction. Institute of Education and Social Development of Beijing Normal University released the *Blue Book of Social System: China's Social System Reform Report No. 7 (2019)*, which did in-depth and detailed research on social system reform and innovation, analyzed the direction of reforms in 2018 and bring forward relevant policy recommendations. Southwest National Education and Psychological Research Center of Southwest University released the *One County, One Strategy Work Guidance Program for Education Poverty Reduction in Very Poor Counties in Tibet Autonomous Region in May* and put forward specific policy recommendations. Centre for Research and Evaluation of Higher Education of Nanjing University released the "Top 100 Best-in-Class Undergraduate Education Quality Rankings" at the beginning of 2019, which became the first report on the quality of undergraduate education in double first-class ranking universities. China Education Improving Institute released the 2018 *China Education Improvement Report* in early 2019, sorted out the shortcomings of China's education improvement, and put forward corresponding countermeasures and suggestions. The 21st Century Institute of Education released *Research Report on Basic Education in Western China* in August and investigated the education situation in the western region and pointed out that the regional gap in rural education in the western region gradually became a new problem of education development of the western region. The 21st Century Institute of Education also released the *Research Report on the Development of China's Educational Public Welfare Field* (2019), which sorted out the development and changes in education public welfare field, making a prejudgment on the participation of social organizations in the education field, and further pointing out the future direction of social organization involving in education. Changjiang Education Research Institute released the *China Education Policy Proposal* (2019 Edition) before the two sessions in March, proposing to deepen the reform of "decentralization of management service" in education field and promoting the modernization of education governance. At the same time, it published the *China Education Yellow Paper*, discussing the issue of high-quality education development and building a strong country through education. It included the hot issues and difficult issues of domestic education and and put forward corresponding policy recommendations. Local education think tanks have also made a number of reports this year. For example, the Hunan Academy of Education Sciences compiled the *Hunan Education Development Blue Paper*, the *Hunan Compulsory Education Quality Test Report*, and the *Hunan Higher Education Vocational Education Quality Annual Report*. Nanjing Education Think Tank of Nanjing Xiaozhuang University published *The Annual Report of Nanjing Education Finance and Education Hot Issues* (2019 Edition) among others.

(4) Greater social influence

In the past year, the social influence of education think tanks has become more and more important. One of them is to guide public opinion through media participation, the second is to communicate think tank ideas through various high-end forums, and the third is to promote Chinese education internationally. At the beginning of 2019, various education think tanks published articles on mainstream papers such as *People's Daily*, *Guangming Daily*, *Chinese Education Daily*, and *China Social Sciences Daily* to discuss the implementation path of China's education modernization 2035. During the two sessions and the subsequent period of time, relevant experts of education think tanks used traditional media and new media to publish relevant views on such issues as education punishment rights, decentralization of management service in education, and the destruction of "five stubbornness". They used the media to expand the dissemination of ideas, which arouse widespread attention in society.

The Chinese Academy of Educational Sciences used the periodical platform of *Education Research* to interpret and analyze policy documents such as education governance and the *Ministry of Education's Opinions on Strengthening Educational Scientific Research in the New Era*, which set an example for all other education think tanks to interpret policy documents from the discipline and theoretical perspective. Some think tanks focused on the use of new media, and used WeChat official accounts to widely disseminate ideas, such as the "Typical Representatives of 40 Years' Chinese Education in Reform and Opening Up" released by organizations such as Changjiang Education Research Institute, and the "2018 China Education Improvement Report" and other articles, which all had about 100,000 times of readings and retweets.

In terms of hosting high-end forums to disseminate think tank ideas, in addition to the relevant high-end forums held Changjiang Education Research Institute Think Tank Alliance, at the end of 2018, the Beijing Academy of Education Sciences held the fifth "Beijing Education Forum" to explore the role of education in urban development from the perspective of urban-education integration. At the end of the same year, the "Education Think Tank and Education Governance Roundtable Forum of 50" hosted by Changjiang Education Research Institute started discussions and exchanges on the theme of "giving priority to the development of education, accelerating the modernization of education, and building a strong country in education" to promote education. The Chinese Academy of Educational Sciences held the "China Education Science Forum (2019)" in April. The forum thoroughly studied and implemented President Xi Jinping's important exposition on education and the spirit of the National Education Conference, co-ordinated the promotion of national education and scientific research, and focused on the modernization of Chinese education, implementation mechanism of cultivating ideals of talents and education evaluation reform among others. At the same time, the Chinese Academy of Educational Sciences aimed to develop this forum into a "strategy source" that leads education reform and innovation, a "think tank" serving national education decision-making, and a "big stage" for collaborative innovation in education and research fronts, so that gradually develop it into china's first-class, world-renowned educational science forum.[1] National Institute of Educational Policy Research of East China Normal University also held the China

---

[1] "China Education Science Forum (2019) was held in Beijing", http://www.nies.net.cn/gzdt/wyxw/201904/t20190418_334753.html.

Chapter 5 Characteristics of Chinese Education Think Tanks in 2019

Education Development Forum in April to discuss population changes and the allocation of educational resources. In June, the China Education 30 Forum and the China Development Research Foundation and other organizations held a "China Child Development Forum" to focus on child development issues. In the same month, the China Thirty Educators Forum, Shanghai Normal University, and UNESCO Teacher Education Center jointly organized the first National Teacher Education Development Forum, which focused on the issue of the construction and development of teachers in the new era. In August, the China Education 30 Forum held the China West Education Development Forum in Tianshui to focus on education reform in the west. Capital Institute for Economics of Education of Beijing Normal University held the China Private Education Forum in August and released the 2019 *China Private Education Blue Book*. The meeting discussed the reform and development of private education in the new era, especially countermeasures for school environment changes after the amendment of the Private Education Promotion Law. In September, the 7th South China Education Summit Annual Conference hosted by the Guangdong Academy of Education was held to implement the modernization of Chinese education 2035 and discuss the education development of the Guangdong-Hong Kong-Macao Greater Bay Area. Most of the above education think tank forums held several sessions, and formed a good brand image and social impact. In November, Changjiang Education Research Institute and the Education Governance and Think Tanks Research Institute of Central China Normal University held the fourth "50 – person Roundtable Forum on Education Think Tanks and Education Governance" at Beijing Foreign Studies University, focusing on issues of education governance mechanism and education governance modernization. The forum invited some leaders of the Ministry of Education and scholars to discuss education governance. In the same month, at the first "Education Think Tank · Xiangjiang Forum" hosted by the Hunan Academy of Education Sciences, the focus was on artificial intelligence and educational change. Experts and scholars such as Lei Chaozi, director of the Department of Science and Technology of the Ministry of Education, focused on school governance models in the new age of artificial intelligence, teachers' role, changes in student learning styles and other relevant issues. In December, the Sixth Annual Conference of the China Education Forum for Thirty Years was held in Beijing with the theme of "Science and Technology Development and Educational Reform". Experts such as Gu Mingyuan, Xu Hui, Zhu Yongxin held discussions on this theme.

In terms of international influence, currently some high-end education think tanks are actively carrying out public relations and diplomatic activities to expand the influence of Chinese education think tanks. In 2019, Institute of Education and Social Development, Beijing Normal University and the Institute for Global Development and Prospects of the Regent College of Oxford University jointly hosted the fourth "Secondary of Education and Social Governance" seminar in Oxford. More than 70 experts and scholars from both China and Britain discussed the theoretical and practical issues of educational reform and social development, integration of production and education, and social governance, which attracted much attention from the international community.

The International and Comparative Education Research Institute of Shanghai Normal University visited more than 40 overseas countries in

2019. Professor Zhang Minxuan, the head of the think tank, went to Paris in November to participate in the 40th UNESCO General Assembly, and participated in the discussion of the work of the UN secondary institutions. At the same time, the center also received visitors and conducted training programs for many international institutions, universities and administrators, including receiving visitors from World Bank's Global Education Practices Bureau and Moscow State Normal University, and undertaking Botswana's Advanced Training Course for Education Administrators. Due to the center's status of being the "UN Teacher Education Center", its influence in the international education arena continues to expand, and it has played an important role in China's education going global and public relations as well as diplomacy. Local education think tanks have also made important breakthroughs in terms of international influence. In October 2019, Jiangsu Institute of Education Modernization and the Russian National Academy of Education Sciences signed a cooperation agreement to jointly conduct a study on "China-Russia Education Comparison and Development Trends in the 21st Century" and held two think tank research results press conferences and "Seminar of Sino-Russian Education Development Strategy Comparison." Upon the invitation of the Chairman of the Russian State Duma Education and Science Committee, the two think tanks held a seminar on "Sino-Russian Development Strategy and Cooperation Communication" at the Russian State Duma Building. It was finally agreed that the think tank research results press conference would be held alternately in Nanjing and Moscow.

Chapter 6　Problems in the Process of Education Think Tank Development

The Fourth Plenary Session of the 19th CPC Central Committee reviewed and approved the *Central Committee of the Communist Party of China's Decision on Adhering to and Improving the Socialist System with Chinese Characteristics*, *Promoting the Modernization of the National Governance System and the Governance Capability*, *Modernization of Systems and Governance Capabilities*. In the dual process of "modernization of governance system and governance capacity 2035" and "education modernization 2035", education think tanks, which are educational governance systems and soft power, will play a more important role. This is not only the need for the coordinated development of new think tanks with Chinese characteristics, but also the inherent need for the modernization of national governance. Therefore, in view of the ambitious goal of modernizing the national governance system and governance capabilities, there are still some shortcomings in our education think tanks. As President Xi Jinping said, "With the development of the situation, the construction of think tanks cannot keep up and adapt. The problem is becoming more and more prominent."

Chapter 6　Problems in the Process of Education Think Tank Development ▶▶▶

(1) Lack of understanding

There are two aspects to this problem. One is education think tanks users' lack of understanding, and the other is education think tanks builders' lack of understanding. The "users" are governments and educational administrative departments. Since *Opinions on Strengthening the Construction of New Type Think Tanks with Chinese Characteristics* was issued, promoting the construction of education think tanks has become an important task for educational administrative departments. The National Education Work Conference in 2014 and subsequent years, have taken education think tanks construction as an important theme. Work on education think tanks construction boomed during these years. Educational and scientific research institutions also turned to education think tanks. Notably, some humanities and social science foundations of the Ministry of Education that emphasize theoretical research spontaneously and orderly turned to problem-oriented education policy research. The term "education think tank" has become the main goal of these research institutions. At the end of 2019, even academic institutions such as the Chinese Society Education of were transformed into education think tanks as requested by higher authorities. Minister of Education Chen Baosheng proposed at the 40th anniversary of the founding of the Chinese Education Society in December, "Chinese Education Society should strive to build a high-level new type of think tank for education, through continuous endeavors."

Although various parties continue to advocate education think tanks construction, the use efficiency of education think tanks is not enough, according to this project. The so-called "use efficiency" means to what extent educational policy-makers refer to the opinions and suggestions of the education think tank in the process of decision-making. Through investigation, it was found that the vast majority of education think tanks have not been used by education administrative departments at all levels. The fundamental reason is that education think tanks lack effective channels for advising and consulting, which made many education think tanks back to the status as academic institutions doing theoretical research. However, in 2019, education conferences were held successively in various provinces and cities, and a series of regional education policies were issued. In this policy-making process, experts and scholars should and must play an important role. However, according to surveys and visits, the role of education think tanks was not fully realized. Except for the provincial and municipal education science institutes, which are involved in the formulation of regional education policies due to their unique administrative attributes, it is almost difficult for university think tanks to take part in the educational decision-making process. Comparatively, university education think tanks bring together more professional scholars, so they should have conducted better research than local educational academies which focus more on micro aspects of education. Of course, the problem is not only from educational administrative departments. Some university education think tanks carry out activities in the way of traditional scientific research institutions and they do not know how to promote marketing and actively connect with relevant government departments. On the other hand, some educational departments have established relevant regulations regarding purchasing services from university education think tanks, so they would rather use

Chapter 6 Problems in the Process of Education Think Tank Development

the subordinate academies and institutes that are easy to use rather than take considerable responsibility for purchasing college education think tank services.

The other aspect of the problem is education think tanks builders' lack of understanding, which refers to the research quality of education think tanks. For a long time, there was a gap between decision-making research and academic research. Traditional academic researchers disdain decision-making research and believe that it is less academic. This view is particularly evident in the transition of educational research institutions to education think tanks. Some academic researchers held that the development of advice and consultation only involves the scope of policy, and policy is mainly concerned about interests distribution which is intellectual pursuit, so the function of think tanks is mainly to study technical or strategic issues. [1]

In fact, think tanks can also generate important academic ideas, such as game theory summarized by Rand Corporation. But in the current situation, it is very difficult for many education think tanks to change from basic theoretical research to decision-making research. On the one hand, it is dependent on the path formed by long-term educational theoretical research. On the other hand, the role of education think tanks hasn't been fully understood and relevant safeguard measures are absent. At present, the construction and development of education think tanks are largely due to the fact that various educational research institutions have gradually turned to policy research in order to implement the spirit of relevant

---

[1] Li Qinggang & Zhaomin, "Reasons why new-type education think tanks fail in advice and consultation and solutions of the problem", *Education Research and Experiment*, No. 6, 2017.

documents. Therefore, some education think tanks are "forced" to transform and they might be unable to produce effective and valuable thoughts but only has the name of an education think tank. In the selection process of this project, these institutions which cannot be counted as real think tanks were eliminated. In addition, some academic and scientific research institutions are still in the slow process of transition, which is the also the case of many social sciences academies. These academies are less strong than universities in terms of academic research and meanwhile less effective than policy-study offices inside government department.[①] Some local educational academies are in similar situation and they only own the name as "think tanks" but hardly serve the role of a real think tank.

(2) The unsatisfactory quality of professional researchers

Since 2019, the poor quality of researchers has become another barrier for the development of education think tanks. There are two aspects of the problem. One is the inadequate number of professional researchers of education think tanks. Another is the unsatisfactory professional level of education think tanks researchers. For the first problem, since the education think tank is a new concept, many institutions have insufficient number of think tanks researchers. Except for institutions like National Institute of Education Sciences, National Center for Education Development Research which have strong talent

---

[①] Li Gang, "Why social sciences academies are enthusiastic about think tank research and evaluation", *Deng Xiaoping Research*, No. 1, 2019.

Chapter 6　Problems in the Process of Education Think Tank Development

reserves, many education think tanks are in the early stages of their development so they don't have enough professional researchers. Some university education think tanks enrich their research teams by recruiting postdoctoral or doctoral students, such as Institute of Education and Social Development of Beijing Normal University, National Institute of Educational Policy Research of East China Normal University, Comparative Education of Shanghai Normal University. These institutions were established quite early and were headed by leaders of the universities so they have advantages in recruiting large numbers of doctoral students. For example, National Institute of Educational Policy Research of East China Normal University launched the special doctoral program of "education decision-making and policy analysis", in which 44 doctoral graduates were study or graduated. In this way, both the number and quality of professionals are guaranteed. However, all the above are individual cases. Not all education think tanks have the guarantee of the number of professionals, and more education think tanks are still relying on a large number of part-time researchers to carry out their work. However, think tanks such as local academies of educational sciences tend to focus more on micro-education research, playing the leading role in curriculum and teaching. Therefore, their professionals are mostly experts on subject education and not so many are experts of macro-policy research. Due to their position, they seldom recruit professionals on education policy, so they don't have many education policy researchers in service.

The other aspect of the problem is the professional level of researchers of education think tanks. According to the investigation, except for some high-end education think tanks, most education think tanks have insufficient professional standards. In the process of "think tank boom", in order to quickly implement the spirit of the relevant documents of the Central Government and the Ministry of Education, many educational academies and universities began to turn the original research institutions to transform into think tanks, but the researchers still had their expertise on basic educational theories, which resulted in the fact that researchers tended to prioritize theoretical studies over practical studies with a lack of realistic problem orientation and hence had difficulty of transforming their research into government decisions.

In this project, the proportion of university education think tanks reached 66%. Based on the research of multiple university education think tanks, we found that although institutions hope to conduct high-quality policy research to contribute to education reform, the problem is a lack of education policy professionals. These institutions have to recruit people who are engaged in basic theoretical research in education and these researchers have innate knowledge in public policy decision-making and lack of experience in quantitative research. In terms of both research methods and research results, they cannot meet the requirement of forward-looking and predictive education think tanks, and they might probably produce low-quality decision-making research and will be hardly trusted by government departments. In addition to the difficulties in the transformation of existing researchers, another problem is that universities currently don't have enough students majoring in education policy which might slow down the progress in talent pool construction of education think tanks. All these are obstacles to the future development of education think tanks.

This phenomenon is also common in local educational academies.

For a long time, these institutions emphasized research on curriculum and teaching, and have not enough talents on regional macro-policy research, so the quality of their research on education policy is not as professional as expected. Comparatively speaking, social education think tanks, due to the flexibility of their mechanisms, they can hire professionals according to needs and more efficiently, so the quality of their work might be slightly better than other types of education think tanks. Admittedly, the problem for the social education think tanks might be the weak connection between the institution and its researchers.

In sum, the inadequate number and low quality of professional researchers are two main difficulties in the process of high-quality development of education think tanks in the next stage.

(3) The problem of management mechanism

The problem of management has persisted. The slow progress of the system reform is mainly reflected in the slow progress of management mechanism. Although the country released management regulations for high-end think tanks many years ago, local governments and universities haven't done much innovative work on the institutional construction of education think tanks, including aspects like the revolving door mechanism, emergency response system, and the use of funds. Many education think tanks are making slow progress because of existing systems. Regarding the construction of the revolving door mechanism, the idea of implementing the system was proposed by many documents issued by the Ministry of Education and other departments. In particular, the *Opinions of the Ministry of Education on Strengthening Educational*

Scientific Research in the New Era issued by the Ministry of Education in October 2019 emphasized again on "establishing a persistent and benign 'revolving door' mechanism, encouraging outstanding scientific researchers to serve in party and government agencies, institutions, state-owned enterprises and other institutions, and hiring administrative leaders, school principals (teachers) and high-level professionals in companies with practical experience and scientific research capabilities as full-time or part-time researchers in educational research institutions". [1] However, there are still not so many examples now. One of the rare cases was one administrative leader transferring to another education think tank. Zhang Zhiyong, the first-level inspector of Shandong Provincial Educational Department transferred to Chinese Education Policy Research Institute of Beijing Normal University, but cases of education think tank researchers transferring to educational administrative departments are even rarer. The cause of this problem lies in the management mechanism. Although the Ministry of Education had the "revolving door" mechanism in place, but the detailed implementation regulations haven't been issued by provincial governments. Meanwhile, as provincial governments are of the same level of the Ministry of Education, it is still uncertain to what extent the provincial governments respond to the policies issued by the Ministry of Education. On the other hand, from the perspective of law, some provisions of The Civil Servant Law have resulted in the absence of regulations concerning how university think tank researchers enter governmental sector which inhibits university think tank researchers

---

[1] *Opinions of the Ministry of Education on Strengthening Educational Scientific Research in the New Era*, http://www.moe.gov.cn/srcsite/A02/s7049/201911/t20191107_407332.html.

Chapter 6 Problems in the Process of Education Think Tank Development

from "revolving"[①]. And to solve the problem the revision of law is needed. In terms of emergency response system construction, the rapid response mechanism of education think tanks in emergency situations is obviously insufficient. Most education think tanks mainly focused on the original research direction due to the transformation problem. When major national and local education policies are introduced, they lack the ability to participate in researching hot issues, could not effectively participate in the discussion of major educational decision-making issues, and could not be involved in this research area. Therefore, they lack the power of forming persuasive narratives so that they are unable to effectively guide research and public opinion progress. And when negative public opinion on education emerges, most education think tanks lack the basis for cooperation with the media and new media, and cannot play a good role in guiding public opinion. For example, at the end of 2019, Nanjing launched a special program of supervising and investigating the illegal schooling activities by compulsory education schools. The inaccurate understanding of the work itself and simplified implementation of regulations aroused strong public criticism on the Internet, but the local education think tank failed to speak up from the perspective of governmental departments on this issue, which was a manifestation of lacking emergency response in the event of a public crisis reaction. Admittedly this problem is still a common phenomenon, and it is urgent for education think tanks in various places to make efforts to solve it from

---

① Li Jing & Liu Hui, "The 'revolving door' mechanism: the innovation of institutions concerning how university think tanks play a role in governmental decision-making", *Educational Development Studies*, No. 7, 2018.

the aspect of system and mechanism construction and deeply participate in various emergency issues.

The reform of the funding system still has not made much progress. At present, national high-end think tanks provide no upper limit for labor costs, but surveys show that the vast majority of education think tanks are still limited by the regulations concerning use of labor and consulting fees, and some university think tanks still insist that at most 10% of the total research funding can be used for labor allowances and expert consultation. This opinion on expenditure makes it impossible to issue funds to temporary overtime staff in this department or temporarily hired personnel in external departments. For example, Anhui Big Data Research Center for University Management, Huaibei Normal University issued the document *Anhui Provincial Key Think Tank Special Funds Management Measures (Trial)*, which clearly stipulates that "the project responsible unit is not allowed to give labor allowances to staff on duty", but many emergency and temporary advisory reports of think tanks are completed by think tank researchers overtime. Such stipulations may stifle the enthusiasm of the researchers; and the total amount of 10% expenditure on labor allowance forces the think tanks to be unable to purchase outsourcing services, which will inevitably affect the smooth development of think tanks in the long run.

(4) The problem of communication and outreaching

Compared with the communication power of political and economic think tanks, there is still a lot of room for improvement for education think tanks. Due to the problem of unclear positioning, many education think

Chapter 6 Problems in the Process of Education Think Tank Development ▶▶▶

tanks are not fully aware of and have not paid much attention to importance of communication power. "Think tank communication is an important factor influencing the development of think tanks, and also an important content for the construction of new-type think tanks."[1] education think tanks should speed up development in this aspect. In terms of shaping the communication image, education think tanks need to learn from political and economic think tanks such as Chongyang Financial Research Institute of Renmin University of China, CCG, and Pangu Think Tanks to create a good communication image for the general public. As far as domestic education think tanks are concerned, take the National Institute of Education Sciences and National Center for Education Development Research as examples. Due to confidential restrictions of their research content, the results of their research are more often presented in forms of internal references, special reports, express reports and other forms to serve party and government functions. Therefore, they might have not paid enough attention to the image building of communication. Although university education think tanks pay great attention to hot topics and have fewer restrictions on various types of communication, they are limited by funding and have little experience in image creation. Except for a few institutes such as Research Institute for International and Comparative Education of Shanghai Normal University, which put much emphasis on image creation, most university education think tanks have not yet paid much attention to this aspect of work. Local

---

[1] Feng Ya & Li Gang, "The current status of new-type education think tanks communication and strategies for improvement—analysis of media influence of CTTI think tanks", *Library and Information*, No. 3, 2019.

academies of educational sciences also have many limits in this regard due to their semi-official status. Social education think tanks are relatively flexible in terms of image formation because they are not restricted by the system, so they have done better work at image formation, such as Changjiang Education Research Institute and the 21st Century Education Research Institute.

In terms of the construction of communication channels, the system is still not fully developed. Many education think tanks are unable to build channels that combine traditional media with new media, such as television, newspapers, websites, WeChat official accounts, Weibo, and Douyin among others. Hence they may fail to have their work reach more audience, and unable to increase social influence. In terms of traditional media communication, the relationship with television and other traditional media is not close enough, and many education think tanks lack visibility. In terms of website construction, the content of many education think tanks does not update throughout the year, and even some education think tanks have not been able to build official websites. For example, as a high-end education think tank, Institute of Education and Social Development of Beijing Normal University does not have an official website, which hinders their communication and outreach. In terms of new media communication, apart from the WeChat official accounts, few education think tanks are active on Weibo, Douyin and international platforms such as Facebook, Twitter, Youtube, Instagram, Tictok and others. This is an obvious weakness compared with American think tanks.

As for the scope of communication, more attention is paid to domestic communication, and there are few successful cases of international communication. According to 2019 *Global Go to Think Tank Index Report* on January 30, 2020 released by the Think Tank and Civil Societies Program (TTCSP) of University of Pennsylvania, among the top 100 think tanks in the world, there were 8 Chinese think tanks on the list, none of which was education think tank. Twenty-seven Chinese think tanks are selected among the top 100 think tanks of big Asian countries (China, India, Japan, South Korea), none of which was education think tank. This shows that the work done by Chinese education think tanks have not been well known to the international community, and their influence on international education governance is limited, so they fail to arouse the attention of the international think tank research community. In the cases of domestic think tanks, only Research Institute for International and Comparative Education of Shanghai Normal University has the title of "UNESCO Teacher Education Center" and can actively play the role of international communication. Communications between other domestic education think tanks and international think tanks are rarely reported. The lack of effective international education think tank communication channels has become an important factor hindering the spread of Chinese education think tanks' thoughts and restricting their functioning in public diplomacy.

Chapter 7 Suggestions for High-quality Development of Chinese education Think Tanks

Achieving the goal of a strong nation in education requires both down-to-earth operations and a forward-looking top-level design. In order to achieve the grand goal of *China Education Modernization* 2035, we need more and higher quality education think tanks to work together and play their roles. Therefore, from the perspective of high-quality development of education think tanks, we believe we should improve our work in the following aspects to strengthen construction and steadily advance the development of education think tanks.

(1) Further enhance knowledge of education think tanks

First, it is necessary to further enhance the knowledge of the builders and help education think tanks to define their own positions, especially to clarify the differences between think tanks and academic research institutions. The "builders" here include not only the head and the builders of the think tank, but also the superiors in charge of education

Chapter 7 Suggestions for High-quality Development of Chinese education Think Tanks ▶▶▶

think tanks. Take the university education think tank as an example. Although the person in charge of the think tank might be very clear about its positioning and goals, obtaining human resources still depends on the support of the university leadership. In this sense, the "builders" include not only the head and the builders of the think tank, but also the superiors in charge of education think tanks. Once the leaders realize the importance of education think tanks, the development of think tanks will naturally go smoothly. Therefore, we suggest that we should further help "builders" engage in learning, training or other activities to understand the value and significance of think tanks, especially their important role in strengthening the country through education, modernizing education 2035, modernizing education governance system and capacity. Specifically, it is advisable that Department of Social Sciences of the Ministry of Education take the lead and set up a "education think tank training community" for the benefit of the whole country, and invite more influential education think tanks such as National Institute of Education Sciences, National Center for Education Development Research, Institute of Education and Social Development of Beijing Normal University, Changjiang Education Research Institute and other think tanks to provide decision-making research courses and other training courses for domestic education think tank leaders. At the same time, researchers from well-known international university think tanks and research institutes can also be hired, and in particular introduce the successful experience of American university think tanks such as the American Education Policy Research Alliance, the University of Illinois at Urbana-Champaign's National Learning Outcome Evaluation Institute, Brown University Annenberg School Reform Institute, Advanced Research Center of Global

Education of Arizona State University, so as to bridge the gap between domestic decision-making research and theoretical research, and accentuate the two-sided relationship between think tank research and disciplinary development. This might alleviate the difficulty university think tanks and local research institutes have when they are turning to do policy research.

In this process, it is suggested that the Department of Social Sciences should recognize the pioneering work of some key humanities bases of the Ministry of Education turning from theoretical research to decision-making and theory. In addition, the training courses should also consider multiple aspects such as the accuracy of decision-making consultation, the brand of think tank products, and the difference in service scope, so as to help think tanks, especially university education think tanks and local academies of educational sciences, be able to adapt to local conditions and times, and be able to produce more effective decision-making research.

Secondly, it is necessary to further enhance the knowledge of the users ofeducation think tanks, especially the education administrative departments' understanding of the value and role of education think tanks. In this regard, education administrative departments at all levels need to seriously study and implement the two relevant documents on the construction of think tanks, and launch learning and training programs at all levels to foster new understandings. Moreover, education think tanks should provide high-quality research results which can be taken and must be taken by policy makers. In this way, understandings of users of education think tanks can be thoroughly transformed. Hence, the quality of education think tank research also to some extent determines understanding of education think tanks users. Think tanks should take the initiative to engage with major government development strategies, focus on forward-looking issues and early-warning issues in education, and be able to submit high-quality decision-making reports in order to achieve the real goal of think tanks. Considering the special nature of think tank management and coordination, we recommend that propaganda departments at all levels can select high-quality education think tanks to be integrated into the unified system of management, construction and evaluation of the Propaganda Department based on local conditions, and build a bridge between the government and think tanks. Therefore application, communication, coordination and evaluation of education think tanks can be taken into a unified system so that resources of education think tanks at all levels can be revitalized and better utilized.

(2) Further strengthen the cultivation of education think tank talents

The output of high-quality educational decision-making research results depends on high-quality researchers who are engaged in educational policy studies. Only when talent cultivation is efficient can the talent team construction and professional level of think tanks be enhanced and it remains the work of universities to prepare large numbers of talents.

In view of the current mode of talent cultivation in education programs in Chinese universities, the first of our suggestions is that universities which are authorized to grant master's and PhD degrees in education should promote the establishment of second-level disciplines in education policy as soon as possible, combine teaching resources of education and management disciplines and carry out education policy programs suitable for local situations. Qualified universities can cooperate with universities that have prepared large numbers of talents, such as Beijing Normal University and East China Normal University, and gradually improve their talent cultivation capacity. In particular, they should learn from the special doctoral program called "education decision-making and policy analysis" offered by National Institute of Educational Policy Research of East China Normal University. The program recruits 10 doctoral students in 2019 from education, demography, sociology, human geography, linguistics, urban planning and other different disciplines. Some universities can copy this model and start with the master's program and then gradually expand the scope and improve the effects. The second is to closely focus on the goals of educational policy research in curriculum setting. In addition to the basic theoretical courses in education, we must continue to emphasize on management courses, including public relations policy, policy analysis methods, comparative education policy, population policy, and quantitative analysis of decision-making to achieve training objectives accurately. Qualified universities can connect the two disciplines of management and education, set up joint curriculum and offer relevant programs. Third, we must strengthen the use of interdisciplinary research methods, especially quantitative research methods, such as education measurement and statistics, policy evaluation and other methods to let data to speak in policy research. In addition to training existing talents on interdisciplinary research methods, it is also advisable to recruit professionals from other disciplines, such as economics, demography, management, and statistics, so as to enhance the plurality of research team and better utilize interdisciplinary research methods. The fourth is to promote research through talent cultivation. It is advisable for institutions which provide training programs to transform into education think tanks during the process of talent cultivation, especially education policy research institute which are authorized to recruit doctoral and MA students. We should learn from the experience of Institute of Education and Social Development of Beijing Normal University, National Institute of Educational Policy Research of East China Normal University, China Institute of Rural Education Development of Northeast Normal University, Research Institute for International and Comparative Education of Shanghai Normal University and promote policy research through talent cultivation. In turn, it is necessary to improve talent cultivation through research and encourage existing researchers to work on realistic educational issues to improve the quality of research. In this respect, local academies of educational sciences and ordinary local colleges and universities, which cannot improve the research team through recruiting young people, can learn from the experience of Changjiang Education Research Institute and other institutions, which continue to launch a series of high-quality research projects and force existing researchers to improve their productivity.

(3) Further deepen the reform of management mechanism

It's necessary to respond to the calls of *Opinions of the Ministry of Education on Strengthening Educational Scientific Research Work in the New Era* and further deepen the reform of the education think tank management system and mechanism and in particular formulate specific regulations and introduce successful experience concerning the construction of revolving door mechanism, emergency mechanism, and funding mechanism.

Regarding the construction of the revolving door mechanism, it is recommended that the Department of Social Sciences of the Ministry of Education take the leading role and and the provincial and municipal education departments formulate specific rules to implement the revolving door mechanism in local areas, and specify personnel exchange methods, exchange time limits, exchange positions, salary and other aspects. In this regard, provinces and cities can learn from the *Guidelines for Strengthening the Construction of New Type Think Tanks in Shanghai Universities* issued by the Shanghai Education Commission that "University teachers to be encouraged to serve governmental positions or encourage research institutions to engage in full-time policy consulting research. Universities should retain 3% of quotas dedicated to supporting teacher turnover. Teachers who work full-time in governments or research institutions should be allowed to have their employment relationship remain the same. Moreover, it is necessary to explore the establishment of annual salary system for special positions or part-time positions to attract outstanding policy researchers from government, universities, research institutions and companies." Constructing the revolving door mechanism of education think tanks is not only the job of local educational institutions. From the perspective of administrative coordination, it would be more convenient that provincial and municipal education departments take the lead to explore in this area.

In terms of emergency response mechanisms, we must guide the development of rapid response capabilities of education think tanks. It is recommended that propaganda departments in various places launch programs that simultaneously train education think tank researchers and news media personnel. This practice has two purposes. One is to make management more convenient. Another is to guarantee that researchers have more channels to led their voice heard when they try to guide public opinions in emergency situations. In addition, it is necessary to establish and improve the evaluation methods of education think tanks, and prioritize emergency projects that require "short and quick response" by the policy-making governmental departments and ensure the availability of qualified researchers in emergency situations.

With regard to constructing funding system, apart from implementing the spirit of the central government's documents on the construction of think tanks, local think tanks should learn from the high-end think tank about funding management mechanism and speed up the establishment of special management mechanisms for education think tank funds. Restrictions on consultation fees and other aspects should be lifted in order to fully motivate think tank researchers. Where appropriate, it is suggested that some university education think tanks can take a step forward to develop the institute as an independent entity, establish independent legal persons and accounts, and achieve autonomy in the use of funds.

In sum, under the current situation of slow progress in the reform of the overall management system and mechanism, we propose to select leading provinces in education modernization such as Jiangsu Province or cities such as Nanjing to set up special zones for education think tanks reforms. We also propose to actively and effectively explore emergency response mechanisms and assessment methods, so as to pave the new road for reform and development of the institutional mechanisms of various think tanks across the country.

(4) Further expand the channels and scope of education think tank communication and outreaching

Education think tanks should adopt a variety of measures to continuously expand the channels and scope of communication and increase the influence of think tanks. First, it is suggested that institutions should build communication image of education think tanks, break the traditional concept of "The smell of good wine will not die out despite the long alleys", and be able to build the public image of think tanks that are responsible and productive. It is possible to build the brand of think tanks through hosting high-end conferences, establishing platforms with the media, and speaking out on hot issues and difficult issues in education. Second, it is necessary to establish communication channels for education think tanks. We must not only cooperate with traditional media, use traditional channels to spread ideas, but also cooperate with new media. Education think tanks can cooperate with traditional television and newspaper media to host high-end forums to fully utilize their respective advantages and jointly expand their influence. At the same time, we must also pay attention to the construction and maintenance of think tanks' official websites, postings on WeChat official accounts, Weibo accounts, and also accounts of Facebook, Twitter, Youtube, Instagram, Tictok and other international platforms and establish a complete set of new media communication system. In addition, we must also pay attention to online marketing, continuously occupying the market through promotion, and use market share to influence public opinions and decision-making dynamics. Chinese education think tanks can learn from the CRM model of American think tanks, such as regularly sending posters of think tank activities to customer mailboxes, regularly holding brand-name forums of think tanks, launching events for registered members, to increase the stickiness of think tank news-feeds subscribers and diversify communication channels. Third, we should expand the scope of education think tanks. Specifically, it is necessarily to strengthen cooperation with international education organizations and international think tanks, such as the the Education and Skills of OECD, Education Global Practice of World Bank, and the Brookings Institution, to formulate research plans ahead of time on relevant educational issues and hold dialogues and high-end forums in order to expand the scope of Chinese education think tanks.

Appendix 1   Events of this Project in 2019

Number	Time	Important Events	Locations
1	2019.1.27	Zhenjiang · Changjiang Education Forum	Zhenjiang
2	2019.3.3	Beijing · Chang Education Forum	Beijing
3	2019.3.19	Press Conference of Chinese Education International Competitiveness Index	Beijing
4	2019.4.27	Chinese Education Think Tank Construction Forum	Beijing
5	2019.6.1	Ningbo · Changjiang Education Forum	Ningbo
6	2019.8.19	Shanghai · Changjiang Education Forum	Shanghai
7	2019.8.25	Tianjin · Changjiang Education Forum	Tianjin
8	2019.9.18	Visit International Monetary Fund (IMF)	Washington
9	2019.9.20	Visit the Brookings Institute, National Public Radio (NPR)	Washington
10	2019.9.20	The sixth Heyuan Peace Day (sponsored by China World Peace Fundation)	Beijing
11	2019.9.26	Visit National Broadcasting Company (NBC)	New York
12	2019.9.27	Visit USA Today	New York
13	2019.9.29	Xi'an · Changjiang Education Forum	Xi'an
14	2019.10.12	Haikou · Changjiang Education Forum	Haikou
15	2019.10.26	Tianjin · Changjiang Education Forum	Tianjin
16	2019.11.9	2019 education think tanks and Educational Governance 50 Educators Roundtable Forum	Beijing
17	2019.12.1	Guangzhou · Changjiang Education Forum	Guangzhou

Appendix 2　Brief Introduction of Changjiang Education Research Institute (CERI)

Strongly supported by the Provincial Education Department of Hubei Province, the Changjiang Education Research Institute (hereafter as CERI), which was sponsored by the Central China Normal University (hereafter as CCNU) and the Changjiang Publishing & Media Group, is one education and research institution founded on 16th December 2006. Zhou Hongyu, member of the standing Committee of the National people's Congress, vice president of the China Education Society, vice president of the China Society for Educational Development Strategy, Deputy Director of the Standing Committee of the People's Congress of Hubei Province, CCNU professor and doctoral supervisor, holds the post of Dean.

Based on the guiding ideology of "Global Vision, China's Position, Professional Competence and Practice Orientation" and the legislative principle of "People's Stance, Construction Attitude and Professional View", the CERI has gathered a group of domestic and foreign high-quality educational experts. A platform has been set up to link relevant education experts and education management departments with the support of cultural publishing enterprises. It has formed a new type of institutional mechanism, which is based on academic research, focused on policy research, supported by publishing enterprises, supported by the government, and supported by social participation, with the complementary advantages of "learning, research, industry, government, and society" and coordinated promotion.

For more than 12 years, the CERI has been working hard to create a new type of educational think tank, "Heavy Apparatus," and strive to turn the "plan" of the think tank into the policy decisions of the party and the government, and the "program" of the think tank into practical actions. The "speeches" of think-tanks have been translated into social consensus and better dedicated to reform. For two consecutive years in 2016 and 2017 of CTTI, the social think tanks MRPA ranked third in the country, and the MRPA resource effectiveness evaluation ranked first in the country. In 2017, he was selected by the Chinese Academy of Social Sciences as the "China Core Think Tank of the year 2017". In 2018, the index of social think tanks in the social think tanks in 2018 PAI rating list of the second in the country. In 2018, the CERI ranked the second in the country in terms of PAI values of social think tanks in CTTI.

Appendix 3 Brief introduction of Research and Evaluation Center for Educational Think Tank and Governance (ETTG)

The Research and Evaluation Center for Educational Think Tank and Governance (shortened as ETTG) focuses on education think-tank, indicators of education think tanks and education governance, and provides education decision-making consultation to government departments, guide public opinion and promote the construction of education think tanks for the purpose of strengthening education. It is headed by Zhou Hongyu, Member of the Standing Committee of the National People's Congress, Deputy Director of Hubei Provincial People's Congress Standing Committee, Vice President of the Chinese Society of Education, President of the Changjiang Education Research Institute, and Professor of Central China Normal University, relying on Central China Normal University in partnership with Changjiang Education Research Institute. It tries to integrate the scientific research resources and talents in an all-round way, aiming at the construction of "China's first-class university education think tank", and striving to build a research and innovation platform with remarkable influence and authority in the field of global education think tank and education governance as well as the evaluation and release center. The center makes full use of the academic ideas and theoretical advantages of colleges and universities and education and scientific research institutions to provide a feasible scheme for the government's strategic decision and third party evaluation.

ETTG carries out research on education think tanks, education governance, indicator and evaluation of education think tanks, education investigation and education policy research. It regularly publishes the ranking of nationwide education think tanks, and provides scientific evaluation data for the development of education think tanks in China; "China Educational Think Tank and Governance 50 Forum" is held regularly each year, bringing together the national education and other related field famous experts tocarry on the discussion exchange on the important education question; It also studies the operational mechanism and characteristics of world-renowned education think tanks, actively participate in the global exchange of think tanks, and gradually expand the visibility and influence of China Education Think Tanks in the international arena. The Center is committed to promoting the construction of education think tanks and the reform of education governance in China, and promoting the international visibility and voice of Chinese education think tanks.

The China Educational Think Tank and Governance 50 Forum (shortened as CETTG50), founded on December 16, 2017, is one of China's most influential non-official, non-profit education think tanks focused on education, policy research and communication. In order to

Appendix 3 Brief introduction of Research and Evaluation Center for Educational Think Tank and Governance (ETTG) ▶▶▶

promote the construction of a new type of Chinese education think tank, the comprehensive reform in the field of education in China is promoted in an all-round way, and the education governance system and the modernization of governance ability are promoted. The full membership of CETTG50 is composed of more than 40 education elite members. In the future, some economists, entrepreneurs and political leaders outside the education industry will be considered as the core members of the forum, which will produce more ideological collisions. CETTG50 is held in November of each year and will be gradually expanded to become a famous forum brand. The forum has been successfully held twice, which has had a wide influence in the field of education and think tanks.

The researchers of the Center have so far published a lot of papers (100 + in key journals), books (20 +) and reviews (200 + in various media), and extensively participated in various education policy consultation activities of government departments. The center has successfully held many forums and activities with Changjiang Education Research Institute Nanjing Xiaozhuang University, Guangzhou University, Shaanxi Normal University and Tianjin University of Science and Technology, etc. In November 2018, CETTG50 was held in Beijing. The "China Education Think Tanks Evaluation System", developed jointly by the Center and Changjiang Education Research Institute and Nanjing Xiaozhuang University, became the first think tank indicator system that describes and collects data of education think tanks in an all-round way, providing users with functions of data collation, data retrieval, data analysis, and data application. *China Education Think Tank Evaluation SFAI Research Report (2018)* was published in the forum, which has had a positive and important impact on the domestic academic circles, and has pointed out the direction of the development and future trend of China Education Think Tanks.

Appendix 4 Constructing Social Think Tanks and Promote National Governance Modernization

In recent years, social think tanks have mushroomed. A number of well-known social think tanks have played an important role in theoretical research, policy advice and consultation, social services, international exchanges among others. Think tanks such as Globalization Institute, China Silkroad Think Tank Research Institute, Pangu Think Tank, Haiguo Tuzhi Research Institute, China Economic Reform Research Foundation, Chahar Institute, and Changjiang Education Research Institute are all very active. According to 2018 *Chinese Think Tank Report* released by the Think Tank Research Center of the Shanghai Academy of Social Sciences, there are 57 social think tanks, accounting for 11.2% of the total number of think tanks. Social think tanks have become an important part of the Chinese think tanks. On January 31, 2019, Think Tank and Civil Societies Program (TTCSP) of University of Pennsylvania released the *Global Think Tank Report* 2018, and a Chinese social think tank was once again selected as "2018 Global Top 100 Think Tanks".

It can be seen that Chinese social think tanks have already made their appearance in the global think tank community. In the main body of China's diversified think tanks, social think tanks, as representatives of folk wisdom and ideas, will certainly play an increasingly unique and important role in the country's decision-making consulting system and public diplomacy. This is not only the need of coordinated development of new-type think tanks with Chinese characteristics, but also the inherent demand for the modernization of national governance.

Enhancing Reform and Opening-up and National Governance Modernization

In the past, social think tanks have made tangible contributions to improve the new think tank system with Chinese characteristics, promote scientific and democratic decision-making by the party and government, deepen national reform and opening up, modernize the country's governance system and capacity, and enhance the country's soft power and national governance modernization. At present, the fourth industrial revolution in the world, featuring digitalization, networking, and intelligence as its main features, comes unexpectedly, and it will profoundly change the inherent relationship between people, people and things, and things and things, and will have a bearing on human society and bring new development opportunities. The task of domestic economic and social transformation is not easy, the contradictions between people's growing needs for a better life and unbalanced or inadequate development are prominent; the fast international wave of globalization, the rising populism, trade disputes, economic turmoil, the digital divide, climate

Appendix 4　Constructing Social Think Tanks and Promote National Governance Modernization ▶▶▶

change and other traditional or non-traditional global issues all put higher requirements on China's reform and opening up and national governance. In this process, as a special force connecting decision makers with society and citizens, social think tanks should have a sense of urgency and mission, focus on the prominent contradictions and problems facing China's development, and conduct in-depth investigations and studies to provide solutions and high-quality policy research results that can address challenges in China's reform, opening up and national governance.

It is the basis for social think tanks to actively engage with national strategic needs in order to seek long-term development. If social think tanks want to pursue long-term development, they need to have both national and a global perspective, and closely integrate their own growth with national strategic needs. In the macro context of China's promotion of high-quality economic and social development, expansion of reform and opening up, active participation in global governance, and promotion of the "Belt and Road" initiative, social think tanks should actively connect with national strategic needs, be problem-oriented and goal-directed, and provide countries with policy products that function as strategic prediction and risk early-warning to meet national development needs. Social think tanks have great opportunities in many aspects including providing construction plans for our own country, making Chinese voices heard by the outside world, propelling the international community's doubts, hesitation and obstacles to the "Belt and Road" Initiative, and building the theory and practice of a community of shared future for mankind and others.

Diversify the Resources of Funds

Think tanks are non-profit and objective. Not-for-profit, or public benefit, is the basic positioning of think tanks around the world. Objectivity requires think tanks to conduct research and consultation independently. China's social think tanks should adhere to the principles of non-profit and objectivity under the premise of serving the party and government; take the perspective of non-governmental professionals, hold the attitude of offering constructive advice, adhere to professional spirit, and be practice-orientated; carry out scientific research to form professional judgments, and do not cater to the needs of administrative departments or interest groups; insist on carrying out empirical research based on evidence, speak with facts and data, and ensure objective and authentic policy research and consultation. The normal operation of social think tanks requires sufficient funds as a guarantee. Diversified sources of funds are an important prerequisite for social think tanks to maintain objectivity. Diversified funding sources can guarantee the objectivity and rigor of the products of social think tanks, so that think tanks will avoid advocating for interest groups, blindly agreeing, or loosing a basic position. At present, China's social think tanks have no shortage of financial support, but the source of funds is still an important factor that plagues the development of social think tanks. As China's think tank product market has not yet matured, it lacks a standardized think tank product supply system. Problems such as a single source of funds, a lack of transparency, a social donation system, and cultural lag have all become threats to the competitiveness and credibility of social think

Appendix 4 Constructing Social Think Tanks and Promote National Governance Modernization ▶▶▶

tanks. Although *Several Opinions on the Healthy Development of Social Think Tanks* clearly proposes to "widen the financing channels of social think tanks and construct a diversified, multi-channel, and multi-level funding security system for social think tanks", the detailed implementation measures have not been nailed down. Relevant departments should start to study and formulate support management mechanism for the sources of funding for social think tanks as soon as possible, including improving the entry threshold for social think tanks, improving the supply and demand system of think tank products, improving the government's purchase of think tank service mechanisms, improving public welfare donations and tax deduction systems, encouraging companies and institutions, social organizations, foundations, and individuals to donate funds to support the construction of social think tanks, and providing corresponding incentive measures and honor systems. The systematic funding support of social think tanks can ensure the public welfare and objectivity of social think tanks to the greatest extent. This is also an important prerequisite to ensure that social think tanks provide effective intellectual support for national reform, opening up and modernization of governance.

Build Bridges between the Government and Non-government Sector

As non-governmental organizations that provide decision-making consultation, social think tanks can open another window for national scientific and democratic decision-making choices. Only when decision-makers are good at absorbing insights from all aspects can they distinguish right from wrong and make decisions more objective and grounded. It is the responsibility of social think tanks to build bridges between the government and people. *Several Opinions on the Healthy Development of Social Think Tanks* states that social think tanks should serve scientific decision-making and assume social responsibilities. They should insist on putting social responsibility first, always adhere to the fundamentals of safeguarding national and people's interests, consciously practice the core values of socialism, and conduct consulting research on issues that are important in the decision-making of the CPC and the government.

Social think tanks come from the private sector and are based at the grassroots level. They have the unique advantage of building a bridge between the people, society and the government, and can effectively connect people's needs with national development. To this end, social think tanks should take root in the people, go deep into the realities and the front line, listen to the voices of the people, understand the real situation, and come up with results or plans of consultation that are practical and effective based on sufficient investigations and data. Social think tanks should become a bridge between theoretical expertise and policy practice, a catalyst that integrates economic, political, social, educational, scientific, cultural, health, environmental and other fields, a link between domestic and global governance theory and practice, and truly become boosters forreform and opening up as well as modernization of state governance. In terms of diplomacy, as an unofficial organization, social think tanks can become an important force in national diplomacy, represent the voices of Chinese society, expressing China's position, China's ideas, and Chinese wisdom on the international stage, fight for the right to speak internationally, and support the country in achieving strategic goals.

(Source: original article published by Zhou Hongyu & Fu Rui on *China Social Sciences Daily*, July 22, 2019)

Appendix 5　How Education Think Tanks Engage with Public Diplomacy

In recent years, the Central Committee of the communise Party of China and the State Council have clearly stated in several documents that think tanks should play a diplomatic role and listed it as one of the five major functions of think tanks. President Xi Jinping has repeatedly emphasized the need to "build a think tank exchange and cooperation network" and promote "think tank diplomacy". When implementing the guiding principles of the Central Committee, some important political, economic, and military think tanks begin to play important roles in international affairs. At this point, there is still much more that education think tanks can engage with.

The document *China Education Modernization 2035* clearly puts forward the strategic task of "creating a new pattern of opening up to the outside world in education sector", and proposes to "actively participate in global education governance and deeply participate in the research and development of international education rules, standards, and evaluation systems." This strategic mission objective is highly aligned with the diplomatic function of think tanks. In the future, education

Appendix 5   How Education Think Tanks Engage with Public Diplomacy ▶▶▶

think tanks will have many roles to play in public diplomacy. It is one of the important channels to tell the story of Chinese education, consolidate Chinese people confidence in their own education, spread Chinese education culture, and help build a community of shared future for mankind.

China Education Think Tank Evaluation SFAI Research Report (2019) clearly states that international influence indicators should cover such indicators as international cooperation, international promotion, and employment of overseas employees. This is not only a review of the diplomatic function of domestic education think tanks, but also an urging call and a proposal for the rapid development of the diplomatic functions of education think tanks. In the current process of constructing and developing education think tanks, different education think tanks still lack international influence. For example, many education think tanks have deficiencies in aspects such as participating in international education affairs, the structure of international education institutions, and cooperation, co-construction, and promotion of international education institutions. This situation is inconsistent with our goals of advancing education modernization and building a strong education nation and needs to be continuously improved.

At present and for the period to come, we must focus on the scope of education think tank diplomacy, seize the key points and steadily expand, not only seize the opportunity to implement the document of the Ministry of Education's *Promoting the Joint Construction of the "Belt and Road" Education Action*. The focus of education think tank diplomacy is the countries along the "Belt and Road", and the task is to meet the educational needs of the countries along the Belt and Road, to form a two-wheel drive of economic and trade cooperation and education development, and to strive to expand the radiation scope of education think tank diplomacy. Through mutual exchanges and cooperation, the ultimate goal is to spread China's education experience to countries around the world. To achieve this goal, education think tanks community should conduct work in the following three aspects.

First, further strengthen cooperation with international education organizations. At present, four Chinese institutions have co-constructed education think tanks with international institutions. Specifically, Beijing Normal University, Shanghai Normal University, Southern University of Science and Technology and Hainan Provincial Education Research and Training Institute, cooperated with UNESCO in constructing International Rural Education Research and Training Center, Teacher Education Center, Higher education Innovation Center, and International Center of Associate Schools. Compared with the goal of "in-depth participation in the research and development of international education rules, standards, and evaluation systems" in *China Education Modernization 2035*, four cooperative institutions are not enough. In the future, we will not only further strengthen cooperation with UNESCO and jointly build related educational institutions, but also strengthen cooperation with comprehensive international institutions such as Department of Education and Skills of OECD, the Department of Education Global Practice of World Bank, continue to expand the scope of cooperation between Chinese education think tanks and the world's top institutions, and encourage these important international education organizations to cooperate with domestic universities and institutes to build think tank platforms, and ultimately Chinese education think tanks can gradually participate in the formulation of rules and standards of international education affairs. At the same time, we also need to leverage the global

Appendix 5 How Education Think Tanks Engage with Public Diplomacy ▶▶▶

influence and outreach of these institutions. We will not only bring new things in, but also use their channels to build education think tanks in foreign countries and expand scope of research and finally enhance the influence of Chinese education think tanks.

The second is to further promote Chinese education in globe. Introducing Chinese education experience to the world is a manifestation of Chinese cultural confidence and comprehensive soft power. Therefore, we must combine the past and the present. First, summarize and promote the successful education experience and methods in Chinese history, especially the educational practices that might be useful to developing countries. For example, Tao Xingzhi's life education theory, whose cores are "life is education" "society is school" "integration of teaching, learning and doing", and "little instructor system", might still be useful models for less developed countries and regions to rapidly improve the quality of education. We can introduce the theory of life education to the countries and regions along the "Belt and Road" through education think tank diplomacy, which can not only help those countries improve the quality of education within a short time, but also introduce China's educators and their educational thoughts to the world. Secondly, we should refine the current highlights and experiences in China's education reform and introduce them to countries around the world, especially outstanding educational models and methods that have emerged in China's education practices over the past 40 years of reform and opening up. For example, the good quality of Shanghai students in the OECD's International Student Assessment (PISA) test attracted worldwide attention, so educational delegations from the United Kingdom and other developed countries came to learn the experience, which was a catalyst of the global promotion of the English textbook *Real Shanghai Mathematics*.

The successful experiences and methods in these education reforms suggest that we can show to the world the advanced part of Chinese education culture. In short, through the combination of the past and the present, we can show the heritage and development of Chinese education, advantages and strengths of Chinese education for a long period of time and promote global communication of Chinese education experience.

The third is to further strengthen training international talents and encourage international exchange of education think tanks talents. According to statistics, 450 Chinese employees served in the United Nations in 2018, accounting for only 1.09% of the total number of United Nations staff. In UNESCO, China shares 5.1% of its membership fees, but only 1.6% of staff members are Chinese. The number of Chinese employees in international institutions such as the World Bank is also less than 2%. Without sufficient Chinese employees to serve in educational departments of important world organizations, it is difficult to achieve our goal of participating in global education governance. Therefore, at present and for a long time to come, we must first train more talents who are qualified to serve in international organizations, especially organizations serving as education think tanks such as UNESCO, OECD, World Bank and other institutions. It is necessary to offer language, education and other related courses in colleges and universities, and set up university departments to train talents who have both global perspective and Chinese values to serve international organizations, and also establish channels to send them into relevant international education organizations so as to lay the foundation of human capital for China's participation in global education governance. Secondly, it is necessary to strengthen the international exchange of education think tank talents. It is recommended that the relevant

Appendix 5 How Education Think Tanks Engage with Public Diplomacy ▶▶▶

international exchange departments of the Ministry of Education and the Ministry of Human Resources and Social Affairs select education policy and education think tank researchers with good language skill from high-end education think tanks to serve positions in Department of Education and Skills of OECD, the Department of Education Global Practice of World Bank and other institutions, understand and participate in the formulation of international education standards and rules. At the same time, it is advisable to actively invite educators from relevant international organizations to give lectures in China, guide the research of educational policies and education think tanks, and jointly train talents through continuous exchanges.

On April 26, 2019, President Xi Jinping pointed out in his speech at the opening ceremony of the second the "Belt and Road" International Cooperation Summit Forum that in the next 5 years China will invite more than 10,000 delegates as representatives of parties, think tanks and non-governmental organizations of countries along the "Belt and Road". This means that the public diplomatic function of Chinese think tanks will play an extremely important role in the next five years. Among all think tanks, education think tanks will also have much to do. Therefore, as researchers and practitioners of education think tanks, we should seize the opportunity and make more efforts in talent cultivation, communication mechanisms, international co-construction, global promotion, and the creation of international educational journals among others to help promote Chinese education opening-up to a new stage.

(Source: original article published by Liu Dawei
on *Chinese Education Daily*, Dec. 5, 2019)